DATE DUE

Arthur Conan Doyle

Twayne's English Authors Series

Herbert Sussman, Editor

Northeastern University

TEAS 451

<small>Sir Arthur Conan Doyle</small>
Portrait by H. L. Gates, courtesy of the
National Portrait Gallery, London.

Arthur Conan Doyle

By Jacqueline A. Jaffe

Indiana University

Twayne Publishers
A Division of G.K. Hall & Co. • Boston

Arthur Conan Doyle

Jacqueline A. Jaffe

Copyright 1987 by G.K. Hall & Co.
All rights reserved
Published by Twayne Publishers
A Division of G.K. Hall & Co.
70 Lincoln Street
Boston, Massachusetts 02111

Copyediting supervised by Lewis DeSimone
Book design by Barbara Anderson

Typeset in 11 pt. Garamond
by Modern Graphics, Inc., Weymouth, Massachusetts

Printed on permanent/durable acid-free paper
and bound in the United States of America

Library of Congress Cataloging in Publication Data

Jaffe, Jacqueline A.
  Arthur Conan Doyle.

  (Twayne's English authors series ; TEAS 451)
  Bibliography: p.
  Includes index.
  1. Doyle, Arthur Conan, Sir, 1859–1930—Criticism and
interpretation. I. Title. II. Series.
PR4624.J28 1987   823'.8   87–8421
ISBN 0–8057–6954–4 (alk. paper)

To my mother, with love,
and to the memory of two
redoubtable Victorian women, Ellen Arnold
and Mildred M. Jaffe.

Contents

About the Author

Jacqueline A. Jaffe received her B.A. from Columbia University and her M.A. and Ph.D. from Indiana University. Her publications include articles on Arthur Conan Doyle's horror stories, Nicholas Monsarrat, and the Victorian sentimental novelists. She is currently teaching at New York University.

Preface

In 1879, when his first story, "The Mystery of the Sasassa Valley," was published in *Chambers* magazine, Arthur Conan Doyle had no intention of becoming a writer. By training and by inclination he was a doctor whose only purpose in writing what he referred to as his "little adventure stories" was to supplement the meager income that a junior member of the medical profession received.

The habit of writing and his continuous need for more money, particularly acute after he had married and started a family, conspired to keep Doyle at work writing short stories and novels in between seeing patients and carrying out all the normal duties of a doctor. For twelve years he would, in fact, combine the functions of doctor and writer. Writing finally proved to be not only the more lucrative but also the more satisfying of his two careers, so that in 1891, when he had at last achieved his medical ambition of an office near Harley Street in London, Doyle saw not one patient because he was devoting all of his time to writing. This was a wise decision, for the man who had said, "I never dreamed I could myself produce decent prose,"[1] then began a career that was to see the publication of more than thirty full-length books, over one hundred and fifty short stories, as well as numerous poems, plays, essays, and pamphlets, and was to establish Arthur Conan Doyle as one of the most successful writers of his age.

The more than fifty years since Conan Doyle's death have seen his literary reputation decline from a position of preeminence to one of relative obscurity. Modern Sherlock Holmes enthusiasts do not merely decline to read Doyle's once famous historical romances, such as *Micah Clark*, or the scientific romances, such as *The Lost World;* they do not even know that these novels exist. And scholars who have been interested in the various genres in which Conan Doyle worked have ignored his longer fiction, preferring to hone their critical skills on the historical romances of Sir Walter Scott or the scientific romances of H. G. Wells. Yet, in spite of this critical disdain, the action scenes in *Sir Nigel, The Refugees,* and *The Lost World* attest to the strength of Doyle's creative gift; they are among the best in English literature. In fact, it is not an overstatement to say that no writer captures the simple joy of action or the zest of an adventure better than Doyle.

If Doyle has been largely ignored as a writer, he has also been neglected as a representative figure of his age, in spite of the fact that many of his own contemporaries found in him the very embodiment of the best of the Victorian spirit. An Englishman, a lieutenant-colonel who hardly knew Doyle personally but who was as familiar with his career as most of the British public, offered the highest possible praise to this Irishman born in Scotland: ". . . Conan Doyle can be accepted as a shining example of the best characteristics of the English race."[2] A friend who was more familiar with Doyle's private life offered a complementary assessment of the writer's personal behavior when he said, "Conan Doyle was the perfect pattern of a gentleman."[3]

Doyle was also an enormously successful public person, who, like many Victorians, believed that it was his duty to participate actively in the social and political events of his time. To this end, he wrote and spoke extensively on a wide range of issues. He was instrumental in the reform of the divorce laws, in the development of the Central Court of Criminal Appeals, and in the establishment of the Home Guard. He invented life preservers for the Navy and secret codes for the Army, and he fought long and hard to turn the cavalry into an infantry that could defend itself with rifles instead of the traditional sabres. Doyle was one of the first people to recognize the danger that submarines posed and the first to warn that in the event of war the Germans would not hesitate to use this new invention.

In his temperament, in his public career, and most especially in his writings, Arthur Conan Doyle summed up the contradictions of his age. Like the Victorian era itself, he looked back with nostalgia on the romantic past of Sir Walter Scott and forward with trepidation to the mechanized future described by H. G. Wells. Similarly, he worked enthusiastically for a liberalization of the divorce laws, while at the same time, and just as enthusiastically, he wanted to deny women the right to vote. In short, Conan Doyle was a serious artist who involved himself fully in the concerns of his time. It is hoped that this study will renew interest in Doyle so he will be recognized in our own time as the major writer his age knew him to be.

In undertaking this volume, I have relied on John Dickson Carr's account of the life of Arthur Conan Doyle as a primary source for biographical information. I am indebted to Carr's book as an example of what a biography should be. I would like to thank Professor Donald Gray for the benefit of his expertise and his unfailing help and support. Thanks are due also to my editor Herbert Sussman, to my friends and colleagues who read and commented on work in progress, to the staff of the Lilly Library at Indiana University, to the ever-helpful and understanding librarians at the Chilmark, Massachusetts, town library, and to Carolyn Heilbrun, who first suggested to me that detective fiction was a valid academic subject.

Jacqueline A. Jaffe

Indiana University

Chronology

1859   Arthur Conan Doyle born 22 May at Picardy Place, Edinburgh, the eldest son of Mary Foley Doyle and Charles Altimont Doyle.

1869   Attends a Jesuit school, Hodder Preparatory, Lancashire.

1871   Attends Stonyhurst School, Lancashire.

1875   Attends Feldkirch School, in Austria, to learn German.

1876   Admitted to Edinburgh University to study medicine.

1879   First short story, "The Mystery of Sasassa Valley," published.

1881   Receives Bachelor of Medicine degree.

1882   Establishes private practice in Southsea, Portsmouth.

1884   Receives Master of Surgery degree.

1885   Marries Louise ("Touie") Hawkins, 6 August.

1886   Completes first novel, *The Firm of Girdlestone,* but does not have it accepted for publication until 1890.

1887   *A Study in Scarlet* published in *Beeton's Christmas Annual,* first appearance of Sherlock Holmes.

1889   First child, Mary Louise Conan Doyle, born in January; *Micah Clarke,* first historical novel.

1890   *The Sign of Four* published simultaneously in the English and American *Lippincott's* magazine. *The White Company* published as a serial in *Cornhill Magazine.* In December Doyle and family leave for Vienna where Doyle intends to study as an eye surgeon.

1891   Returns from Vienna and sets up as eye specialist. July to October, first series of six Holmes stories published in the *Strand* magazine. Second series of six continues the following year.

1892   *The Refugees, The Great Shadow,* and third series of twelve Holmes stories. Second child, Alleyne Kingsley, born in November.

1893   Death of Holmes in "The Final Problem" published December, *Strand* magazine. Death of father, Charles Doyle. Onset of Touie's tuberculosis. Family moves to Davos, Switzerland.

1894   *The Stark Munro Letters.*

1896   *The Exploits of Brigadier Gerard; Uncle Bernac.* Returns to Hindhead, Surrey.

1897   *The Tragedy of the Korosko;* a book of ballads, *Songs of Action.* Meets and falls in love with Jean Leckie on 15 March.

1898   *A Duet, with An Occasional Chorus.*

1899   *The Croxley Master.* Boer War begins 11 October.

1900   *The Great Boer War.* "Some Military Lessons of the War" in *Cornhill Magazine.* Serves for seven months at Bloemfontein Field Hospital, South Africa. Stands for Parliament, is defeated.

1901   *The Hound of the Baskervilles* begins appearing in installments in the *Strand.*

1902   *The War in South Africa: Its Cause and Conduct.* Knighted 9 August, at Buckingham Palace.

1903   *The Adventures of Gerard.* "The Adventure of the Empty House," depicting the return of Holmes in October. This series of Holmes stories published continuously until December 1904.

1906   *Sir Nigel.* Stood for Parliament, defeated. Death of his wife on 4 July. Begins detective work on case of George Edalji.

1907   Marries Jean Leckie 18 September.

1909   "The Crime of the Congo." Birth of a son, Denis Percy Stewart, in March.

1910   Begins detective work on behalf of Oscar Slater. Birth of son, Adrian Malcolm, in November.

1911   Begins Spiritualist writings with *Through the Veil.*

1912   *The Lost World;* "The Case of Oscar Slater." Birth of fifth child, Lena Jean Annette, in December.

1913   *The Poison Belt* and "Great Britain and the Next War."

1914   *The Valley of Fear* and "Danger." Continues work on Oscar Slater case. After war is declared, 4 August, establishes prototype of civil defense unit.

1917 Declares himself a Spiritualist.

1918 *The New Revelation.* Death of son, Kingsley, of influenza following war wounds.

1919 *The Vital Message.* Death of brother, Innes, from pneumonia. Begins extensive traveling and lecturing on behalf of Spiritualism.

1921 *The Wanderings of a Spiritualist.* Death of mother, Mary Foley Doyle.

1922 *The Coming of the Fairies.*

1924 *Memories and Adventures,* autobiography.

1925 *The Land of Mist.*

1926 Two-volume *History of Spiritualism.*

1927 Final Holmes story, "The Adventure of Shoscombe Old Place." Achieves release of Oscar Slater.

1930 Dies of a heart attack 7 July at his home, Windlesham, Surrey.

Chapter One
The Pattern of a Gentleman

The determining influence of Arthur Conan Doyle's childhood, and much of his adult life, was that of his mother, Mary. From the moment of his birth on 22 May 1859, Mary Foley Doyle was totally devoted to her eldest son, and his devotion to her seems to have been encouraged beyond what is usual by the fact that his father, Charles, a withdrawn, melancholy man, largely absented himself from family affairs. As time went by, Arthur had to take on more and more of the responsibilities that his frail father could not fulfill.

Charles Doyle was the unfortunate youngest son of a talented, staunchly Catholic family. Charles's father and Arthur's grandfather, John Doyle, was "H.B.," one of the most influential political cartoonists of his day. Arthur's grandfather had also been a force in London life; such influential friends as William Makepeace Thackeray, Sir Walter Scott, Benjamin Disraeli, Samuel Taylor Coleridge, and William Wordsworth all made regular appearances at his dinner table. Two of Arthur's uncles, James and Henry were extremely successful in their chosen careers, while a third, Richard ("Dicky") Doyle, eventually rivaled his father's fame as a satirist and caricaturist.

But the youngest boy, Charles, who wanted to be an architect, never progressed beyond his first job as a builder and designer with the Public Works Office in Edinburgh. Charles suffered from epilepsy, emotional disturbances, and from comparison with his famous father and prosperous brothers so that, as time went by, he retreated more and more from public life. Eventually, his melancholia became chronic, and his family had to commit him to a mental institution. Later, in a forgiving moment, Arthur, who had often felt bitter about his father's desertion of his familial responsibilities, would describe Charles's life as "full of the tragedy of unfulfilled powers and of undeveloped gifts" (*MA*, 25).

Mary Foley Doyle, the stronger personality and more active parent, was determined that Arthur's powers and gifts should not be wasted. To this end, she spent innumerable hours with her son reading, explaining, and tutoring him in all the things that she felt

1

he needed to know to be a cultured gentleman. These lessons were all colored by Mary Doyle's obsession with questions of ancestry and lineage. By the time he was ten, Arthur could recite his family's line back to the Plantagenets and could blazon a shield with the heraldic symbols of any of his ancestors. He was further encouraged by the stories of heroic actions and adventure that his mother recounted while she worked around the house. Combining the unknown with the known, weaving the actions of the paternal Doyle and maternal Foley ancestors around the deeds of great men and events of history, these stories presumably captured both the storyteller and the listener.

This intermingling of family narrative with history and folktales also helped form in Arthur a passionate and personal attachment to the past that he was never to lose. Further, as Mary's stories of knight-errantry always emphasized the moral framework within which heroic action must take place, Arthur learned to believe that one man or group of men could shape events in the cause of good. Indeed, the connecting theme of all of this instruction, and fundamental to Mary's point of view, was the nature and responsibilities of chivalry. Under his mother's tutelage, and in an atmosphere that was, he later reported, "entirely feudal to a degree unknown to the ordinary flow of life,"[1] Arthur Conan Doyle developed an interest in genealogy, history, and adventure that he would pursue through his life and in all his writings.

When Arthur was ten, he was sent to Hodder House, a Jesuit preparatory school for the famous Jesuit college at Stonyhurst in Lancashire. Both of these schools were authoritarian and rigid. At Stonyhurst, of which Arthur said the "curriculum, like the building, was mediaeval but sound" (MA, 9), he studied elements [chemistry], figures [arithmetic], rudiments [geometry], grammar, syntax, poetry, and rhetoric in a spartan environment where good behavior was rewarded by the addition of a piece of meat given with the usual supper of hot milk, bread, and butter.

Arthur's love of adventure, his energy, and a nature that "rebelled against threats and took a perverted pride in showing that it would not be cowed by violence" (MA, 10), all combined to make him the recipient of much of the priests' displeasure. But, although Arthur hated the coldness, the rigidity, and the injustice of such a system of education, he seems also to have welcomed the discipline and the structure that the Jesuits provided. Much as he disliked their system, he tried to use it as a touchstone against which he could test himself. In later years Doyle was to sum up his experience at school thus: "The boys made it a point of honour not to show that they were hurt by any aspect of life at Stonyhurst and this suppression was the best training for a hard life" (*MA,* 11).

The tales told to Arthur in his childhood also helped him bear these school years. In fact, they seem to have played a greater role in the formation of his character than his studies because it was while he was at Stonyhurst that he became a gifted storyteller. Since his favorite childhood author had been Mayne Reid, the American writer of boys' adventure stories, and his favorite book *The Scalp Hunters* (1856), the plot of that adventure story provided the jumping-off point for many of the stories of adventure set in foreign lands that he told his schoolmates. Yet, however much he borrowed from Reid, he always added his own moral lesson to these tales; the correct rules for fighting, the correct attitude for dealing with the female sex, the correct behavior in the dangerous situations was always emphasized.

The pleasures of narration, while great, could not extinguish the normal interests of a twelve-year-old, for, as he later explained, "I always stipulated for tarts 'down' before I began the latest episode."[2] The skills that he had learned at home provided him with friends, with something to eat, and with a way to spend his time. He was, he said later, a spinner of yarns even then.

For his final year before entering medical school, Conan Doyle went to Feldkirch School in Austria. Since the conditions at Feldkirch were humane in comparison to those at Stonyhurst and the teachers were kinder, Conan Doyle's year abroad was a pleasant one. His year was not entirely without incident, however, for at some point during this period his studies appear to have undermined some of his inherited faith. It was during his year away from home that he began to question his belief in Catholicism. His interest in rationalism and the use of the intellect, which was later to be channeled by his work at medical school into a lifelong interest in scientific methods of investigation, put him naturally in opposition to any system based on faith alone. His resolve to be a genuine scientist led him to insist on experimental verification for everything.

Religious thought was not exempt from this scrutiny, so Catholicism had to make sense, had to fit the facts as they were empirically known, in order to satisfy him. An unverifiable, ephem-

eral notion of faith was clearly not enough. His movement away
from Catholicism was not the product of a sudden decision on his
part, and he did not yet make a definitive break from the Church,
but this time of doubt marks a turning point in Doyle's life.

Nineteen years after Feldkirch, in 1894, Conan Doyle published
The Stark Munro Letters, an autobiographical account of his time of
spiritual doubt. The book is structured as a series of letters between
the agnostic, J. Stark Munro, and his friend, Bertie Swanborough,
a devout Catholic. While the Munro letters do express a yearning
for a solution to the questions of the universe, the discussion is
dominated by Munro's insistence on the use of reason as a way to
find that answer. At one point Munro, who at first chides his friend,
breaks into an impassioned defense of his belief in reason: "Can't I
hear your grave voice saying, 'Have faith!' Your conscience allows
you to. Well, mine won't allow me. . . . 'The reason cannot help
in such a matter,' you reply. I answer that to say so, is to give up
a battle before it is fought. My reason *shall* help me and when it
can help no longer I shall do without help."[3]

Doyle intended to apply this position to all organized religions,
not just to Catholicism. Although his initial experience of religious
intolerance was naturally directed against members of his own faith,
first the Jesuits and later his father's family, he quickly applied the
test of reason to other religions and found them wanting. As he
recorded again in *Stark Munro*: "I have mastered the principles of
several religions . . . Their ethics are usually excellent. So are the
ethics of the common law of England" (*SM,* 18).

Arthur did not lose his belief in God, however. He was not then,
nor would he ever be, an atheist. He resolved his religious struggles,
which began in Feldkirch and were to continue for the next three
or four years, by deciding to break free of hierarchical religion and
to become, in his own words, "a respectful agnostic" (*MA,* 64). As
an agnostic, he replaced the strictures of the Jesuits with an inclu-
sive, universal god, who, as a beneficial power, was present everywhere and in everything. Like many Victorians, Arthur Conan Doyle
believed that nature made it impossible for a rational man to be an
atheist, for nature was "the true revelation of the Deity to man"
(*MA,* 145). He saw in the freedom of nature a promise of a similar
freedom of spirit for mankind, a spirit which could not be contained
or explained by the rigid dogmas of Catholicism. He was not an
acknowledged member of any organized group, but his feelings

about the majesty of nature bordered on the religious, so that the pantheist doctrine, which says that the universe taken or conceived as a whole is God and that the combined forces and laws that are manifested in the existing universe are God, is a fair description of his position at that time.

The depth of Doyle's disillusionment with traditional systems was measured two years after his crisis of faith when he was trying to decide where he should set himself up as a doctor. At his mother's insistence he went to London to consult his influential uncles and aunts. Before he went, though, true to his ideals of strict honesty, he wrote to tell his relatives of his doubts about the Catholic Church. His Aunt Annette replied with the suggestion that he come to London to explain his position to them. Unfortunately, he could offer no explanation that could satisfy them, and a bitter quarrel ensued. Conan Doyle felt that he was being asked to compromise his conscience and his reason, while the family felt that Arthur was endangering his very soul.

Doyle refused to write about that occasion, so we have no record of his initial response to the family argument. Later, however, in *The Stark Munro Letters,* he described—fictionally—what he would have said. At the beginning of the book, when the Catholic alter ego counsels Munro on the virtues of faith, he responds: "I see so clearly that faith is not a virtue but a vice. . . . Yet you would counsel a man to shut out that far more precious gift, the reason, and to refuse to use it in the most intimate questions of life. . . . I tell you, *I* cannot do so" (*SM,* 12).

After this rift with his father's family, the depth of which only his mother seemed to understand, Arthur had to fend for himself. All the offers of social connections and financial help that he had depended upon were withdrawn. Only once more did his childless aunt and uncles make any effort to help him, and that offer was again premised on the hope that he would turn out to be a Catholic "at heart." Since it was precisely "at heart" that Arthur was now an agnostic, the overture was refused, and Conan Doyle set up in private practice in Portsmouth without any of the letters of introduction necessary to launch a successful medical practice. He was impoverished by this rift in many ways, the most pressing of which was that he was often so poor that he could not afford a meal.

He did have plenty of time and imagination, however, and he used both of these to write short stories. While still a medical student, he had worked at a number of jobs, the most adventurous being two stints as a ship's doctor, first on a whaling vessel to the Antarctic and second, on an African freighter. He had dutifully sent the money earned home to his mother, but the real value of these trips only became clear when he needed material to put in his stories. Drawing on these diverse experiences, he began to write adventure stories about obsessed, haunted people set against the background of the ice floes of the Antarctic or the steaming jungles of West Africa.

Many of these stories, including such ultimate successes as "The Haunted Grange of Goresthorpe" and "The American's Tale," were initially rejected and would not be published until years later, but a sufficient number were accepted to encourage Conan Doyle to continue. He tasted his first success when "The Mystery of the Sasassa Valley" was accepted by *Chambers* magazine in 1879, and was made even more hopeful by the acceptance of "Bones" and "The Gully of Bluemansdyke" by *London Society* in 1880 and 1881. But his first professional success and perhaps the most heartening came in 1884, when the prestigious *Cornhill* magazine accepted "Habakuk Jephson's Statement." Not only did the public like it, but, perhaps more important to the emerging writer, James Payn, the redoubtable editor of *Cornhill,* approved of both story and author.

After Conan Doyle had been in practice for two years, and while he was doing more writing than doctoring, he met Louise Hawkins, the woman who was to become his wife. He does not seem to have fallen passionately in love with her nor was she the woman he was to love best. But she needed him and she looked to him for help and guidance, and this seems to have mattered more than passion to a man like Doyle, trying to live according to a knightly code. Touched by her position and relieved of his loneliness by her proximity, Doyle seems to have made a rational decision to get married.

The couple met when Louise's only brother Jack became suddenly ill. The first doctor whom Louise and her widowed mother consulted diagnosed cerebral meningitis. As the case was so grave, Doyle was called in to give a second opinion. Seeing immediately that there was no hope of recovery, he invited the Hawkinses to bring Jack to his house. The intention of this act was twofold: as a doctor he wanted to be able to attend the boy at a moment's notice, as a man he felt that he had to take care of the two women who were alone and helpless with a seriously ill family member dependent on them.

Jack Hawkins died a few days later. The funeral was held from Doyle's house, and Louise Hawkins and Arthur Conan Doyle were married within a matter of months.

The affection that they felt for each other, formed in a time of crisis, seems never to have wavered. Their marriage lasted from 1885 until Touie's death from tuberculosis in August 1906. After her death, Doyle was to describe Louise as "a girl who was full of such smiling patience, that no man could have had a more gentle and amiable life's companion" (*MA,* 65). Characteristically, Doyle would never discuss his wife or his marriage in any other terms. The "amiable" companion was his friend, as the phrase suggests, and the depth of his need for another kind of relationship, a passionate, intimate one, would only be expressed later, in the context of his love for the woman who was to be his second wife, Jean Leckie.

Arthur Conan Doyle's early marriage gave strong impetus to his literary career, however. Speaking of the stability of his new domestic life, he claimed that "it quickened both my brain and my imagination." (*MA,* 67). In addition to supplying him with inspiration, marriage also provided him with the leisure to write. Since Louise had a small fixed income of her own, the young doctor's poverty was somewhat relieved, and he had the time to try something he had long been anxious to attempt —a full-length detective story.

Although he preferred adventure stories, as a student he had read and liked Wilkie Collins's *The Moonstone.* He reserved his highest regard, however, for the works of Edgar Allan Poe. While still in medical school, he had read "The Gold Bug" and "The Murders in the Rue Morgue" aloud to his family. Now he reread them, finding in Poe's stories a treatment of the mysterious within a structure of scientific reasoning that particularly appealed to him. Using Poe's stories as a reference point, Doyle invented his detective, a man whose intelligence was so superior to that of his fellowmen that he was able to solve the deep mysteries that ordinary men ascribed to the agency of the supernatural.

Doyle knew from the first that *A Study in Scarlet* was good, yet the first four or five publishers did not seem to think so. After months of delay, Ward, Lock & Co. offered him twenty-five pounds for the entire copyright if they could print it in their Christmas annual for 1887. Doyle was both disappointed and disheartened by this offer, not only because the amount of money was very small, but, more importantly, because he had felt that *A Study in Scarlet* might "open a road for me" (*MA,* 70) and now this opening was delayed. Yet the surge of creative energy that had produced that novel was not diminished by the wait. Doyle describes his subsequent mood as one of optimism: "I felt large thoughts rise within me. I now determined to test my powers to the full and I chose a historical novel for this end" (*MA,* 70). Again, he used this novel to explore questions that he was personally considering, questions of religious freedom and the dangers of fanaticism, for example. *Micah Clarke* was finished early in 1888 and was immediately rejected by every publisher it was sent to. Meanwhile, *A Study in Scarlet* was out but was not attracting the attention that its author wanted. Once again, Conan Doyle decided to give up writing and to devote his energies to becoming an eye surgeon, and once again he was distracted from his medical ambition when *Micah Clarke* was accepted by the chief editor of Longmans Publishing Company, Andrew Lang.

It is to Andrew Lang that Arthur Conan Doyle owed his career as a writer and his first major success. In his autobiography, *Memories and Adventures,* Doyle describes the public's reception of *Micah Clarke* thus: "I have never forgotten it. . . . It was the first solid cornerstone laid for some sort of literary reputation" (*MA,* 71). *Micah Clarke* did indeed prove to be the cornerstone, for from its first appearance in print, both critics and readers were enthusiastic in their praise. Triumphant notice followed triumphant notice until even the author was convinced of his book's success.

Meanwhile, contrary to its British reception, the Sherlock Holmes novel had been doing very well in America, so well in fact that Conan Doyle was asked by an American agent to write another Holmes adventure to be published complete in one issue of *Lippincott's.* Doyle promised to do so, even though he was writing another historical novel, the book that was always to be his favorite, *The White Company.* In between chapters of *The White Company* Conan Doyle quickly wrote *The Sign of Four,* which was to be published in the United States in the spring of 1890. Although the Sherlock Holmes fever had not yet really begun, the author of *Micah Clarke* was now an established writer, and as such he was becoming a public personality. Asked to speak at the Saville Club, to be interviewed and photographed for local newspapers, to attend the "Idlers" dinner where he met J. M. Barrie for the first time, Doyle was beginning to taste the fame that was never afterward to leave him.

During the next year the public's interest in Sherlock Holmes continued to grow. In 1891 Conan Doyle wrote six stories featuring the detective, which were published consecutively by the *Strand* magazine. These were so popular that by December 1891, four years after Holmes's first appearance, the detective had assumed the status of a fairy-tale hero. Holmes was so popular that many people refused to believe he was fiction, and his name often eclipsed that of his creator. Letters, telegrams, and parcels addressed to Sherlock Holmes, Esq., were duly delivered without delay and to Doyle's continuing chagrin to Arthur Conan Doyle. People wrote to inquire after Holmes's health, to send him their favorite recipes, to argue with his readings of the evidence, and to beg Dr. Watson to publish more stories about his friend and mentor.

At first Doyle was amused by this attention but then, as the pressure to produce more and more Holmes stories continued, he became infuriated. He found the narrative demands that the stories made on him an intolerable burden. He could not, he said, "afford to spin plots at such a rate. They are apt to become thin and break." Further, he had made a vow: "never again to write anything which was not as good as I could possibly make it, and therefore I would not write a Holmes story without a worthy plot and without a problem which interested my own mind" (*MA*, 92). At last, after doing two series of twelve stories in two years, he decided that he was in danger of "being entirely identified with what I regarded as a lower stratum of literary achievement" (*MA*, 93). In April 1893 he decided to kill Sherlock Holmes at the Reichenbach Falls.

Fortunately, Conan Doyle and his wife were abroad when the story telling of Holmes's death appeared in print. The shock to the public was so great that one of Doyle's biographers, Charles Higham, reports that "not until the death of Queen Victoria seven years later was there such widespread mourning."[4] While this may be an exaggeration, there certainly was an enormous outpouring of grief and protest. As dramatic evidence of the extent of the national dismay, twenty thousand people immediately canceled their subscription to the *Strand*, while tens of thousands more wrote to the editor, the publisher, and the author to complain. Many readers mourned, and the queen herself was rumored to be upset.

Nevertheless, for a long time Doyle resisted the pressure to res-
urrect Holmes. He turned his attention to the historical novels that
he loved best, to scientific romances, to plays and poems, to newspaper articles, to touring America, to wintering in Egypt for his
wife's health, and to building a new house at Hindhead, Surrey. It
was not until seven years later in 1901—after the Boer War, his
abortive stand for Parliament, and the death of the queen, when
Doyle felt that the era of the Victorians was over and the world
would never be the same again—that he succumbed to public demand and wrote *The Hound of the Baskervilles*. While not exactly a
resurrection of Holmes, because the story was set at some time
before Holmes's meeting with Moriarty, *The Hound of the Baskervilles*
set the stage for what was to come when, in 1903, ten years to the
month since he had met his end, Holmes reappeared in a new series
of short stories.

By the time of Queen Victoria's death in 1901, Arthur Conan
Doyle had achieved a great many of his youthful dreams and aspi-
rations. At the age of forty he seemed to have everything that he
had ever wanted. In addition to *Micah Clarke* and *The White Company*,
he had written and published six other full-length historical novels.
He had authored two volumes of stories of adventure and mystery,
the autobiographical *Stark Munro Letters* (1894), a novel about a
modern marriage titled *A Duet: With Occasional Chorus* (1898), a
contemporary adventure called *The Tragedy of the Korosko* (1897), a
collection of patriotic ballads, and two plays. All this, as well as
the Sherlock Holmes novels and stories made him one of the most
prolific writers of an age not known for its literary brevity.

These years also saw a growth in Conan Doyle's reputation as a
forceful public speaker and an influential initiator of social action.
In 1894 he had traveled to Switzerland and to the United States on
lecture tours in which he mingled observations on the state of the
world with readings from his literary works. From Switzerland he
returned with an enthusiasm for skiing and from the United States
he came home with an undying affection and respect for Americans.
From that time on he was a self-appointed champion of the United
States, no matter what the dispute or difference of opinion between
the two countries might be. He believed that the two English-
speaking nations should support each other because they shared a
common heritage and their natural linguistic alliance would inev-
itably bind them together in times of trouble. Doyle was so sure

of this position that in 1900 he wrote a long essay called *An Anglo-American Reunion* in which he warned that if "the essential relationship"[5] between the nations was not actively fostered neither empire would attain the level of greatness that both united could reach.

As his position on America and on several other international issues demonstrates, Doyle was not a chauvinist. He was, however, a patriot. When the Boer War began in 1899, the forty-year-old writer was one of the first civilians to try to enlist. For several months his age defeated him in his efforts to enter Her Majesty's service, but he eventually managed to secure an appointment as medical director of a privately endowed field hospital in Bloemfontein. Doyle set this hospital up and operated it successfully for many months under the worst possible conditions. The South African sun was fierce and there was little or no shade outside the sweltering tents. In addition, the facility was chronically understaffed and overused; frequently there was not enough water, and wounded and doctors alike were subjected to periodic devastating attacks of enteric fever. Much of the credit for the success of this hospital was due to Conan Doyle's skill and his seemingly ceaseless energy.

Having been an on-the-spot witness to the conditions under which the British soldier was being asked to fight, Doyle decided he could best continue to help the war effort when he returned home by writing a pamphlet explaining the causes of the conflict and defending the conduct of British troops from the constant attacks to which they were subjected in the European press. In January 1902 Conan Doyle published *The War in South Africa: Its Cause and Conflict,* a pamphlet that sold thirty-five thousand copies in England alone during its first six weeks in print. As a result of this work, and the full-length history that preceded it, a number of influential foreign newspapers tempered their decidedly anti-British rhetoric.

In May 1902, as a mark of the government's recognition of the service that he had performed, Conan Doyle was offered a knighthood. True to his notion of honor, he initially refused the title, declaring that "all my work for the state would seem tainted if I took a so-called 'reward': it may be pride and it may be foolish, but I could not do it."[6] When he eventually did accept, he did so at his mother's insistence and for her sake. His real feelings about the title, however, are probably best expressed in a story he subsequently wrote called "The Three Garridebs" in which the heroic Sherlock

Holmes refuses a knighthood on 15 June, the same calendar day that Doyle had accepted his title.

At the age of forty-three, Conan Doyle was one of the most famous writers in the world. He was also an important public figure, a man of political as well as literary clout. There remained one part of his life, however, that was still unsettled, even in the midst of his apparent respectability, and that was the part related to the woman he loved. From the time they had met, Conan Doyle had always felt the deepest respect and affection for his wife Touie. But in 1897, twelve years after his marriage, he fell passionately in love with Jean Leckie, a beautiful twenty-four-year-old woman. There remains no immediate record of how they met, nor any explicit acknowledgement of the intensity of their feeling for each other in the early part of their relationship because, as Doyle succinctly says, "there are some things which one feels too intimately to be able to express" (*MA*, 215). He acknowledged only that their daily correspondence lasted the ten years from the date of their meeting until 1907, when Doyle married Jean Leckie exactly thirteen months after the death of his first wife.

The modern reader frequently finds the delicacy surrounding many Victorian love affairs peculiar and hard to fathom. The relationship between Conan Doyle and Jean Leckie provides just such a case, for while the affair was a passionate one, it was conducted so honorably and with such tact that the writer's wife and children were apparently never aware of it. For the last thirteen years of her life Touie Doyle was ill with tuberculosis, and for those same thirteen years her husband and Jean Leckie wrote to each other almost daily and saw each other whenever it could be arranged. Yet Doyle apparently conducted this affair in a manner that he felt was consistent with his position as a married man.

To his relatives who knew Jean Leckie he repeatedly stressed that their relationship was a platonic one and would remain so; to his mother, who needed no such reassurance, he admitted only that his forbearance was a strain. As a writer, though, Doyle was able to turn his frustration to good account. His relationship with Jean provided him, he said later, with the inspiration to write *A Duet,* his novel about marriage, and with the creative energy to complete his exhaustive history of the war in South Africa. "It is a high and heaven-sent thing, this love of ours," he wrote to Jean. "It has kept my soul and my emotions alive."[7]

While his relationship with Jean and the care of his ill wife occupied much of Conan Doyle's private life during these years, the major intellectual interest of his middle age was taken up by the investigation of psychic matters. As early as 1887, while he still lived in Southsea, a patient had spoken to him of Spiritualism—religion that espouses the existence of a world inhabited by the spirits of the dead—and had suggested that life after death could be proven by testing the spirits who spoke through "mediums" or "guides." Doyle was so intrigued by the possibility of contacting the other world that he read every book he could find on the subject (seventy-four in one year) in an effort to establish the veracity of such reports. The evidence he gathered at the time left him skeptical, but he was so intrigued by the possibility of this approach to the question of life after death that he continued to keep up with developments in the fields of psychic inquiry.

To the contemporary observer it seems almost inevitable, given Conan Doyle's character, that he should have been drawn to Spiritualism. Ever since his student years in Germany he had searched for a system of belief that would make sense of the universe, that would connect the seeming contradictions in a world that frequently rewarded the unjust and punished the virtuous. His agnosticism never provided him with the philosophical center he so anxiously sought; it merely cleared the ground so that some other religious dogma could eventually take root. What that other system was to be was not clear to Doyle for a long time, but as the years went by he became more and more convinced that Spiritualism could answer the cosmic questions that plagued him. He originally sought the demonstration of the power of the spiritual world in the phenomenon of telepathy, but his interest soon led him to witness manifestations of ectoplasm—a fleshlike material produced by the mediums that forms itself into a shape resembling the "body" of the dead spirit—to observe the transmission of verbal messages from beyond the grave, and to experiment with automatic writing and table writing. By 1916 he had so given himself over to the mysteries of the spirits that he dedicated the rest of his life, along with his name and his fortune, to the advancement of the Spiritualist cause.

Although Doyle's belief in Spiritualism, and his proselytizing for greater acceptance of spiritual phenomena was often ridiculed by both his personal friends and by the general public, he never wavered in his faith in the power of the spirits. Just as in the earlier rift with his relatives over Catholicism, he would not compromise his beliefs, no matter what the cost. He thought that what he gave up did not, finally, count for as much as what he gained by following his conscience. To the end of his life he was content to work for Spiritualism, and to regard himself as "an instrument so fashioned that [he] had had some particular advantage in getting the teaching across to the people" (MA, 339).

On 7 July 1930 Arthur Conan Doyle died of a heart attack at his home in Surrey. Several days before his death he had expressed most forcefully the strength of his faith in an afterlife when he announced: "I have had many adventures. The greatest and most glorious awaits me now."[8]

In spite of their suspicion regarding his Spiritualist preachings, the public was truly shocked to learn of his death. The expression of grief was so overwhelming that the Doyle family had to hire a private train to convey all the flowers, letters, and telegrams from London to the funeral in Surrey. Conan Doyle, it turned out, had made friends and helped people all over the world. Further, his books had been read by thousands of people who felt that the creator of many of their favorite characters was as familiar to them as any member of their family. Of all the thousands of messages that the Doyle family received after Arthur's death, perhaps the one that can best serve as his epitaph came from his lifelong friend and theatrical collaborator, J. M. Barrie. "There can never," he wrote, "have been a more honorable man than Arthur Conan Doyle."[9]

Chapter Two
The Writer at Work:
The Early Short Stories

In his autobiography, *Memories and Adventures,* Doyle explains why in 1879 he decided to write fiction: "It was in this year that I first learned that shillings might be earned in other ways than by filling phials. Some friends remarked to me that my letters were very vivid and surely I could write some things to sell." If we are able to take his word and rule out the possibility that such an avid reader always harbored literary ambitions, Doyle's acute need of shillings and his friends' timely advice were the two factors that started him on his way to becoming one of the most successful writers of his age.

In 1878 Doyle, as a third-year medical student, could only earn a very small salary for a short time in between his studies. His financial problems were aggravated by the fact that he was the eldest son of a large family, most of whose members were not yet able to work, and who looked to him to provide them with some financial help. His years as a student and the subsequent ones as a doctor trying to establish a practice were thus colored by his constant anxiety about money. His financial situation, in fact, was only alleviated in August 1885, when he married Louise Hawkins, a woman with a small fixed income of her own which offered some relief from the rigors of genteel poverty.

Doyle was fortunate in that he turned to writing at a time when there was an increasing demand for fiction. This demand from the general public for more and more stories was fueled by various changes in publishing methods, the most important being the introduction of mass-circulation magazines. Such magazines as the *Strand, Longmans,* and *MacMillans,* luxuriously produced on glossy paper with rich-looking illustrations, appealed to an increasing readership with a seemingly insatiable appetite for fiction. Magazine circulation continued to grow all through the 1870s and 1880s so that when, in 1879, Doyle decided to send off his first story "The Mystery of the Sasassa Valley" there were a number of new and prestigious magazines willing to look at the work of an unknown author. At his first attempt, *Chambers* magazine bought the story for £3.3.0, a sum that can be appreciated by comparing it to the two pounds per month that he earned as a full-time medical assistant to a general practitioner.

This propitious start was not to be a true indication of Doyle's early success at publishing, for many of his later stories were rejected by all the magazines that he sent them to. However, he did manage to sell enough stories so that he could feed himself and pay his bills. He later described this period as one in which, "literature . . . was a deciding factor in my life for I could not have held on and must have either starved or given in but for the few pounds which Mr. Hogg [the editor of *London Society*] sent me" (*MA,* 60).

Although Doyle first put pen to paper for financial reasons, he never conceived of himself as a writer of potboilers. He was far from being a contriver of tales who might deliberately fashion a story so that it would sell well. Doyle had a great natural urge to tell stories and being able to write them simply made public what had been, up until that time, a private satisfaction. As he phrased it, "the general aspiration towards literature was tremendously strong upon me . . . and my mind was reaching out in what seemed an aimless way in all sorts of directions" (*MA,* 24). Moreover, while he did not conceive of himself as a good writer, he was sure that the stories of mystery and adventure that had held him spellbound as a child were exactly what the public wanted to read.

According to his contemporary, George Saintsbury, Doyle's desire to write this kind of fiction made him part of an important movement just beginning to make itself known in 1880, when there occurred "an inexplicable rise . . . of diverse persons whose talent inclined in a new direction." For the distinguished literary historian this new breed of writer both created and encouraged "a demand for romance, for historical romance, and for the short story."[1] Although Saintsbury does not mention Doyle by name, it is clear today that he was an important member of this innovative group.

The Romantic Mode

Since tales of adventure and heroism were an integral part of Conan Doyle's childhood and played a very strong part in the formation of his imagination, it is not surprising that he wrote stories in that vein. Although the romantic novel of the sort that interested Doyle was in decline—as Saintsbury says, "It is certain that for about a quarter of a century, from 1845 to 1870, not merely the historical novel, but the romance generally did lose general practice and general attention,"[2]—there continued to be, stretching out over the first three-quarters of the century, a strong group of writers who remained intensely interested in romance.

These writers, who included Bulwer Lytton, Sheridan Le Fanu, Edgar Allan Poe, Charles Reade, Rider Haggard, and Robert Louis Stevenson, together had kept the form of the romance alive. Thus in the 1880s what Robert Kiely terms "a small but vigorous countermovement" to the prevailing forces of realism was emerging under the leadership of Robert Louis Stevenson.[3] These writers took exception to Emile Zola's "insistence upon [the] fall of the imagination"[4] because they felt, as their chief spokesman, Stevenson, so clearly explained, that the imagination was one of the last defenses of creativity.[5]

Romance and Robert Louis Stevenson.   Robert Louis Stevenson was and continued to be one of Doyle's most important models; he held both Stevenson's philosophy and his writing in great esteem. His regard for Stevenson as a theorist is evident from the similarity of their literary concerns and the coincidence of certain themes in their works. His respect for Stevenson as a craftsman can be more clearly seen in the obituary Doyle wrote for the *National Review* in which he describes Stevenson, along with Poe and Hawthorne, as one of the three greatest short-story writers of the nineteenth century.[6] Even the personal philosophies of Stevenson and Doyle were remarkably similar; they both felt that physical activity verging on actual hardship was intrinsically exciting, and that this excitement imposed a reality of its own that was more important than internal motivation, or, as Robert Keily says of Robert Louis Stevenson, that "motion counted more than direction."[7] Furthermore, they both felt that the power of the imagination was supreme and should be used to transport the reader away from the all-too-grim reality that comprised everyday life. Certainly Stevenson's comment, "As I live I feel more and more that literature should be cheerful and brave spirited, even if it cannot be made beautiful and pious and heroic," could be taken as Doyle's own dictum.[8]

Rationalism and Doyle.   Yet there remained the one crucial difference between Doyle and the romantic writers; as a doctor much of his adult life had been devoted to precisely the kind of scientific experimentation and analysis that the realists advocated. In Doyle's case, though, his training as a doctor served only to strengthen his belief that scientific methodology comprised only one approach, one tool which may or may not be useful as a way of understanding human experience.

Doyle himself cites an example of the way that the practice of medicine forced him to recognize the limits of the scientific approach. It was early in his career, and he had just been called in by a poor woman to attend someone in her family, when, as he tells it, "I picked up a candle and walking over I stooped over the little bed, expecting to see a child. What I really saw was a pair of brown sullen eyes, full of loathing and pain which looked up in resentment to mine. I could not tell how old the creature was. Long thin limbs were twisted and coiled in the tiny couch. The face was sane but malignant. 'What is it?' I asked in dismay when we were out of hearing. 'It's a girl,' sobbed the mother, 'She's nineteen' " (MA, 63).

Doyle concluded that those medical and psychological aspects of the girl's condition that he tried to contain in the phrase "loathing and pain," were well beyond the comprehension of the doctor, the scientist, or the student of human nature. The passion, the hatred, and the physical pain that the crippled girl felt could not be measured or dissected in any laboratory and could not be contained in any scientific equation. As a rationalist who wanted to tell romantic tales, Doyle concluded that while the movement to verisimilitude and accuracy of description was useful to the scientist and the doctor, the author and the student of human nature should always remember that what was analyzable was not all that was conceivable.

The Writer

Doyle's early experience as a fashioner of magazine stories was instrumental in the final shaping of him as a writer. He learned much about the art of writing and his talent continued to develop as he continued to practice his craft. These early stories are not all good, although some are very entertaining indeed. Their interest to the contemporary reader lies in the emergence of what were to be characteristic themes in Doyle's work: the heroic code of behavior with its attendant costs and benefits, a love of physical action, an emphasis on male camaraderie and friendship, and a delight in adventure and excitement.

Doyle's writing is also an attempt to invent or impose coherence within the boundaries of the finite entity that is narrative. His portrayal of the heroic code and his archetypal protagonists who subscribe to or violate that code are all attempts to give meaning to the chaos that he believed lay just beneath the surface of existence. As Northrop Frye has pointed out, the romance is "the champion of the ideal," a form which imposes this order.[9] Doyle was drawn to stories of adventure and romance because he wanted a fictional world more hopeful, more heroic, and more moral than the real world and because he was attracted by a fictional form whose structure gave coherence.

First attempts. "The Mystery of the Sasasssa Valley," "The American's Tale," and "The Gully of Bluemansdyke" (published in 1879, 1880, and 1881 respectively) were all inspired by and modeled on popular Bret Harte stories. Doyle calls them "feeble echoes of Bret Harte" (*MA,* 57), but they are better than that. "The Mystery of the Sasassa Valley, a South African Story," is presented by a first-person narrator as a true account of his adventure. The storyteller, Jack Davis, is one of two young men who have left England to search for fame and fortune in South Africa. Initially the two school friends, one English, one Irish, have no success, but just as they are about to return to England, they are told a story by a traveler who has seen a one-eyed ghost in a valley that, according to native superstition, is haunted. The Irishman, Tom Donahue, deduces that the one eye must be a diamond that glows in a strange, lifelike way when it is struck by moonlight. After convincing Jack that they should search for it, Jack and Tom start out and, one false trip and a series of adventures later, find the diamond and ensure their prosperity.

"The American's Tale" is also presented as a true story by someone who witnessed the events. Set in the American West, the story concerns a giant man-eating plant, like an enormous Venus's-flytrap, which, fortunately, snaps up the villain just as he is about to bushwack the young English protagonist. The notion of a large plant that could devour a man was a familiar one to the Victorian reader, for it appeared over and over again in a variety of popular articles that dealt with the wonders and sensations of nature. Doyle's version of the machinelike plant is an especially terrifying one, however, as he has his victims impaled on long spikes hidden inside the leaves before their flesh is devoured.

The third story, "The Gully of Bluemansdyke," set in the Australian outback, deals with a young man's coming of age while riding with a posse that is tracking down a band of vicious murderers. The trooper, Jack Braxton, has already proved himself to be a courageous and skillful tracker, but in this story, he has to learn to accept the help of an older and more experienced woodsman before they can capture the entire gang.

Central to Doyle's first stories is the notion of a strong male friendship that operates as part of a heroic code of behavior. This is less evident in "The American's Tale" where the friendship between the protagonist and narrator is only part of a general background of male friendship and fighting against which the horror of the man-eating plant can be more clearly detailed. Indeed, the clanlike aspect of the men in the American West seems totally insignificant in light of the decisive action that nature takes. But in the other two stories male camaraderie is more explicitly detailed. The protagonists are connected by such a strong bond of sympathy that their relationship goes beyond the normal bonds of friendship; they are blood brothers. Even the generational competition that exists between the brash young Braxton and the older, more experienced woodsman in "The Gully of Bluemandsdyke" is not sufficient to change the nature of the bond that links them.

The friends in "The Mystery of the Sasassa Valley" are also strongly linked in spite of various differences, the most obvious being that Tom Donahue is Irish and Jack Davis is English. In this story the cultural differences of English and Irish are translated into a distinction that was to become familiar to the Victorian reader in the relationship between Mr. Holmes and Dr. Watson—the distinction between an ordinary person, the narrator, and his extraordinary friend, the hero. Jack, who tells the story, is a loyal, kind man of average intelligence. His friend Tom is a man of visionary intelligence, mercurial, decisive, and active. Like Dr. Watson, Jack is fully sensible of his friend's talents. When Tom embarks on what appears to be an incomprehensible course of action, Jack comments: "I had, however, seen so many proofs of my friend's good sense and quickness of apprehension that I thought it quite possible that

Wharton's story had a meaning in his eyes which I was too obtuse to take in."[10]

Like Holmes, once Tom had perceived the truth, he will not stop until the mystery is solved. When their first effort to find the diamond fails, the uncertain and fearful Jack wants to give up: " 'There is no diamond here,' I said, 'Let's return and get a nights sleep.' " (*Gully*, 236). But the impassioned Tom will not let them rest, " 'Let's have one more try,' he said, 'I believe I've solved the mystery' " (*Gully*, 237). In ways like these, the two friends, who foreshadow the partnership of Holmes and Watson, illustrate the special closeness of male camaraderie.

That this masculine bonding takes place best in faraway places, free from the restraints of social conventions, is no surprise. For Doyle, as for most adventure-story writers, the charm of exotic lands lies in their freedom from the demands of a known place in the present time. Society's constraints, in particular the demands of domesticity, have to be removed so that the emphasis can fall, where it rightly belongs, on individual male action and adventure. Doyle's stories are thus set in unknown places or in places that are intentionally geographically vague, like the American West.

Having chosen the adventurous place, Doyle does not have his hero go alone into that timeless country. He puts men together (either as a pair, or as members of a small group) as comrades and blood brothers to illustrate best how the heroic code works. Doyle uses the adventure convention of out of time, out of place to emphasize the permanent nature of male comradeship, and to show how it develops and sustains the participants under every kind of condition. The emphasis is still on individual action, but in Doyle's case the action directly benefits the male familial group, not the male alone, as well as presumably indirectly benefiting the larger society left behind.

First success. Doyle achieved his first critical success in July 1883, when *Cornhill* magazine bought his story "Habakuk Jephson's Statement." Doyle wanted the accolade of being accepted by James Payn, the demanding editor of that prestigious magazine. He also desperately wanted to be in the company of other writers that he admired, and the *Cornhill,* formerly edited by Thackeray, and the publication that had printed Edgar Allan Poe's stories and, more recently, the works of Robert Louis Stevenson, provided access to this inner sanctum of literary excellence. James Payn, "the warden," as Doyle described him, "of the sacred gate" (*MA*, 72), was to be a mentor whose influence was to be felt in all Doyle's work for most of his life. As an early indication of Payn's standing with Doyle, he tells us that "[what] for the first time made me realize that I was ceasing to be a hack writer and was getting into good company was when James Payn accepted my short story" (*MA*, 67).

Although "Habakuk Jephson's Statement" was published anonymously, some of the reviews suggested that Stevenson had written it, a suggestion which was to Doyle, "great praise" (*MA*, 68) indeed. There was another kind of notoriety that developed around "Habakuk Jephson's Statement," however, the kind more readily associated with an Edgar Allan Poe story. "Habakuk Jephson's Statement" is a tale that purports to explain the real-life mystery of the abandoned ship, the *Mary Celeste*. Unfortunately, or fortunately as it turned out, a Mr. Flood, Her Majesty's Advocate-General at Gibraltar, read the story and mistook fiction for fact. He first sent off a telegram to the newspapers calling the story "a fabrication,"[11] and followed this up with a written report to the government which was also circulated to the newspapers.

A taste for writing.   The publication of "Habakuk Jephson's Statement" marked a turning point in Doyle's career. Payn's approval meant that he was becoming a good writer. The publicity following Mr. Flood's pronouncement meant that, like Poe, who had deliberately set out to write a story that would mislead the public, he could write fiction so well that some people would read it as fact. As a result of this experience "he began the year 1884 in a fever of writing."[12] And when, in August 1885, he married Louise Hawkins, the sister of one of his patients, his domestic happiness and now financial security only further fueled his desire to write. As he explained it, "with the more regular life and the greater sense of responsibility, coupled with the natural development of brainpower, the literary side of me began slowly to spread until it was destined to push the other entirely aside" (*MA*, 66).

The Tales of Terror

Although Doyle continued to write adventure stories, the fervor of his new burst of writing led him to explore a genre that he enjoyed as much if not more: the supernatural tale of terror. Some of his earlier works like "The American's Tale" and "The Gully of

Bluemansdyke" play with the possibility of a supernatural explanation for the mysterious happenings, but this suggestion is part of the foil against which the superior human intelligence of the adventurers can come into play; in fact, the existence of devils is disproved in these adventure stories. In his horror stories the situation is reversed. Doyle treats the supernatural seriously. His tales of terror are not, as Charles Higham points out, "what one would expect from the pen of a young, uncomplicated extrovert," [13] but they show an important side of Doyle's character. The heroic and optimistic world of adventure in which a mystery is used only to "intensify and complicate a story of triumph over obstacles"[14] is replaced, in the tale of terror, by a mystery so powerful and terrifying that Doyle confronts not only the limitations of heroic action but "the limitations of mortality."[15] Furthermore, his Gothic tales of mystery and terror, often ending in madness or death, express the darker side of the writer's vision and suggest depths to his character that are not quite evident in his seemingly open and frank memoirs.

It appears as if once having espoused the value of action, and the clarity of the sequential form of the adventure story, Doyle could then freely explore the power of the psyche by allowing it to range freely, unfettered by any code of heroic idealism or social behavior. The need for action and the clarity that action brings are set aside in these mystery stories for the clarity that is achieved only when feelings dominate the intellect, when the single-mindedness of the emotionally obsessed determines all behavior. The protagonists of Doyle's tales of terror all demonstrate this steadfast purpose. Nicholas Craigie in "The Captain of the Pole-Star," Sosra, in "The Ring of Thoth," Cowles in "John Barrington Cowles," and Ourganeff in "The Man from Archangel" are all strange, solitary men dominated to the point of insanity by a singular fixation—their love for a dead woman. And like the earlier Gothic protagonists that these characters so clearly resemble, they fail in their various attempts to overturn the natural order because they are finally consumed by their obsession.

"The Captain of the 'Pole-Star.' "   "The Captain of the 'Pole-Star' " (published in *Temple Bar* magazine, 1883) is the first of these tales that Charles Higham explains, "reach beyond the boundaries of normal experience into a no man's land between life and death."[16] Set on a whaling ship bound on a hazardous journey into the frozen Arctic, this story, which begins in a manner strongly reminiscent

of Mary Shelley's *Frankenstein,* uses material that Doyle collected in
a diary while he was on a similar voyage. However, Doyle embel-
lishes his experience by portraying the captain of the *Pole-Star,*
Nicholas Craigie, as a man haunted by the spectre of the dead woman
he used to love. She is a sirenlike figure, who calls to him and
beckons him and the ship further and further into the middle of
the treacherous ice floes. Several members of the crew hear the ghost
crying, but she is visible to no one except the captain. This vision
separates the captain from the society of the men with whom he
travels, producing moments of desperate isolation. " 'Look!' he
gasped, 'There, man, there! Between the hummocks! Now coming
out from behind the far one! You see her—you *must* see her!' "[17]
Finally, the captain keeps his tryst with his lover: " 'Coming, lass,
coming,' cried the skipper in a voice of unfathomable tenderness
and compassion,' " while he runs "with prodigious speed" (*Polestar*
31-32), across the ice and into her arms. The captain's passion for
his long-lost love transcends the natural boundary between life and
death, for when the crew members find the captain's frozen body,
they see the shape of a woman, fashioned out of "little crystals of
ice and feathers of snow" ("The Captain of the Pole-Star", p. 35)
bending over the corpse to kiss it. As the crew reports, this reunion
has made Craigie happy, even in death; "Sure it was that Captain
Nicholas Craigie has met with no painful end, for there was a bright
smile upon his blue, pinched features and his hands were still out-
stretched as though grasping at the strange visitor which had summoned him away into the dim world that lies beyond the grave"
(*Polestar* 34).

"**The Ring of Thoth.**" A refusal like Craigie's to accept the
fact of physical death also characterizes the Egyptian, Sosra, in "the
Ring of Thoth" (published in the *Cornhill* in 1890). In this tale, a
student of Egyptology, John Vansittart Smith, is mistakenly locked
in the Louvre at night when he falls asleep while studying the
mummies. He is awakened by an approaching light from a lantern,
carried by an attendant who Smith has noticed earlier because he
bears a marked physical resemblance to the ancient Egyptians. "It
was indeed the very face with which his studies had made him
familiar. The regular, statuesque features, broad brow, well-rounded
chin, and dusky complexion were the exact counterpart of the innumerable statues, mummy cases and pictures which adorned the
walls of the apartment. The thing was beyond all coincidence"

(*Polestar*, 292). While Smith watches, the attendant unwraps one of the mummies and embraces what appears to be the perfectly preserved body of a beautiful young woman.

In the confrontation that follows the Egyptian's discovery of Smith, Smith learns that the attendant, Sosra, was a priest of Thuthmosis, who lived sixteen hundred years before the birth of Christ. During his priestly studies Sosra had discovered a wonderful potion that gave eternal life. After Sosra had swallowed this potion, he met and fell in love with a beautiful woman, Atma, and she returned his love. But before he could convince Atma to take the mixture and join him in life eternal, she fell ill and died. Since her death, Sosra has been searching for the ingredients for another potion that would counteract the first and enable him to "shake off that accursed health which has been worse to me than the foulest disease" (*Polestar*, 314).

Sosra finally finds the potion that he has so long sought in a ring—the ring of Thoth—which was hidden in Atma's burial garments. Vansittart leaves and Sosra drinks the liquid while clasping the unwrapped Atma in his arms. As in "The Captain of the 'Pole-Star,' " when the lovers are found in the morning, Smith reports that "so close was his embrace that it was only with the utmost difficulty that they were separated" (*Polestar*, 315).

"John Barrington Cowles." Published in 1886, "John Barrington Cowles" is a story of a man who, like Sosra and Craigie, dies for love; however, in this case, the love is misplaced. A handsome and sensitive young man, John Cowles suddenly falls in love with a beautiful but mysterious woman, Kate Northcott. No one seems to know who she is, where she comes from, or what her past contains. The narrator, a medical student and close friend of Cowles's, tries to find out about the woman, but he is only able to uncover some unsavory rumors about her former lovers. The narrator does, however, know that Kate is a strong-willed and determined young woman, for he sees her one day cruelly punishing her little dog "with a heavy dog whip." the dog "shining piteously" ws "evidently completely cowed" (*Polestar*, 242).

Although the narrator tells John to give Kate up, the obsessed Cowles proceeds with his plans for an early marriage only to discover on his wedding eve that his bride-to-be is a creature so terrible (some form of vampire is hinted at) that her true nature cannot be revealed. Indeed, the knowledge alone is so terrible that it is enough to drive Cowles to the edge of madness. In a vain attempt to recover his sanity and to escape from Kate's influence, Cowles and his friend travel to Scotland. But the spectre of Kate Northcott haunts Cowles wherever he goes, calling to him and allowing him no sleep, until one moonlit night, unable to bear his obsession any longer, he breaks free from the restraining arm of his friend, runs to embrace Kate's beckoning figure, and plunges over a cliff to his death.

This story is the first one in which Doyle shows the obsessional object to be evil. In "John Barrington Cowles," Doyle explores, as Charles Higham explains, "The Gothic writer's feelings of terror about women, who are often portrayed as vampires, luring men to doom,"[18] in a way that reverses the pattern of Doyle's other tales of terror. Craigie, Sosra, and Ourganeff, the protagonist of "The Man from Archangel," all actively seek death because it will reunite them with the women they love, and—happily—break the power that their obsession holds over them. These characters are only waiting for the right signal from beyond the grave so that they can go to the death that they welcome. By contrast, John Cowles tries to escape from Kate and to break free from her relentless embrace. But he is unable to do so, perhaps because this obsession is imposed from outside and thus involves forces beyond the power of his own will. Kate is too strong, too determined to have her own way, and too imbued by supernatural powers to be challenged; the sensitive Cowles is broken by that combination.

"John Barrington Cowles" demonstrates the voluptuous nature of the loss of control. There is a sensuous quality in Cowles's inability to act that implies that, at least in this story, Doyle finds total passivity attractive. Cowles is, interestingly, the most effeminate of these possessed men, the one who bears the least resemblance to what Kiely calls that "darkly masculine race of nineteenth-century demon-heros: Manfred, Melmoth, Rochester . . . Heathcliff,"[19] who are his literary predecessors. Cowles, who is slight and fair, handsome but frail, is in contrast to the strong, passionate Craigie and Sosra.

A more important distinction between the two kinds of obsessional stories lies in the fact that Cowles is innocent. He is the passive victim of evil, whose innocence is shown to be dangerous, for it renders him powerless. The attraction of passivity is here linked to a warning about the naiveté that leads to such a surrender. Unlike Craigie, Sosra, and Ourganeff, who maintained the ability to act throughout the story, Cowles is never heroic. He is always the victim, never an instigator. The sexual element in Cowles's surrender to Kate should not obscure the warning implicit in the story: naïveté and innocence are not admirable qualities, for they lead to passivity, powerlessness, and death.

"The Man from Archangel." In another and more interesting fictional experiment, "The Man from Archangel" (1885), Doyle tried to find a way in which he could portray a protagonist ruled by passion in a story that would question his obsession. "The Man from Archangel" was one of Doyle's own favorite stories, for it was, he said, "perhaps as good honest work as I have ever done" (*MA,* 67). It is also especially interesting, in the light of the other stories, for the way it questions the grand gesture of surrendering one's life to a fixed desire. Doyle achieves this double purpose of exploring the nature of an obsession and suggesting an alternative to it by dividing his Gothic hero into two, the doomed lover, Ourganeff, and the narrator, M'Vittie.

M'Vittie is a misanthrope who removes himself from society by going to live in a small cottage on a bleak tract of land next to the sea in the Scottish Highlands. M'Vittie is a scientist who has committed his life to a search for the answers to certain scientific questions. He is also a romantic in the tradition of Manfred, Heathcliff, and Ballantrae, all of whom were embittered by the puny nature of modern man, and were portrayed, as Robert Kiely points out, as part of the "myth of a lost giant in an uncongenial world."[20] M'Vittie is such a character, except that he is not contemptuously taking the world on: he is contemptuously leaving it to its own mediocrity.

M'Vittie establishes his life in such a way that he can continue his experiments while seeing no one and speaking to no one. This continues until one day, during a violent storm, a ship is wrecked at sea and a beautiful Russian girl, Sophie, is washed upon the beach next to his cottage. M'Vittie reluctantly gives her food and shelter and learns that she has been abducted from her wedding to a "soft-skinned boy" (*Polestar,* 133) by Ourganeff, the captain of the doomed ship, a man who had been Sophie's intended husband until he was presumed lost at sea. The captain is obsessed by Sophie and has vowed not to live without her. M'Vittie, the obsessed scientist, insists that such a passion for another human being is incomprehensible to him.

Apart from their choice of obsessional objects, though, the two men are remarkably similar. They are physically alike—tall, dark, and very strong—and also alike in their personalities—determined, active, and inordinately proud men with violent tempers. Sophie's obsessed lover, Ourganeff, has forcefully abducted Sophie from her wedding, and M'Vittie has fled to the Highlands because: "I had nearly slain a man in a quarrel, for my temper was fiery and I was apt to forget my own strength when enraged" (*Polestar*, 109–110). Their duality is actually established at their first sight of each other. M'Vittie sees the ship go down and catches a glimpse of a man who is behaving differently from the other sailors: "He was a tall man who stood apart from the others, balancing himself upon the swaying wreck as though he disdained to cling to rope or bulwark . . . He stood dark, silent and inscrutible looking down on the black sea and waiting for whatever fortune Fate might send him" (*Polestar*, 117).

When they meet face to face, they find that they are physically similar: "I suddenly became aware of a shadow which interspersed itself between the sun and myself. Looking around, I saw to my great surprise a very tall powerful man who was standing a few yards off" (*Polestar*, 126). Except for the fact that they are obsessed by different passions, M'Vittie by his experiments and Ourganeff by Sophie, the two men are mirror images of each other. At the end of the story Ourganeff once again abducts Sophie and drags her from her rescuer to a death that only the lovers can share. In the aftermath of another violent storm, M'Vittie finds their bodies: "It was only when I turned him over that I discovered that she was beneath him, his dead arm circling her, his mangled body still intervening between her and the fury of the storm." (*Polestar*, 140).

The ending to the story of Ourganeff and Sophie is the traditional romantic one of love conquering death: "I fancy that death had been brighter to him than life had ever been" (*Polestar*, 140). But "The Man from Archangel" is interesting not for the expected death of the lovers but for the life of M'Vittie. In this story Doyle has divided his obsessed protagonist into two, one dominated by his love for a woman and one dominated by his love for science, so one manifestation of the usually doomed Gothic hero is left alive. M'Vittie's love for science and for rational explanations to mysteries is clearly the safer, more productive passion.

Yet his encounter with Ourganeff has taught him something about human nature, so that after the death of the lovers, his misanthropy is abated. In a gesture that emphasizes his change of heart, he allows wild flowers to be put on the graves of the lovers. "No cross or symbol marks their resting place, but Old Madge puts wild flowers upon it at times and when I pass on my daily walk and see the fresh blossoms scattered over the sand, I think of the strange couple who came from afar and broke for a little space the dull tenor of my sombre life" (*Polestar,* 141).

Although M'Vittie's experience with the passion that one human being can feel for another alters him and makes him more sympathetic to the human plight, his passion for scientific experimentation is unabated. In this sense, his story runs counter to those of Dr. Frankenstein and Dr. Jekyll, those other nineteenth-century men of intellect whose pursuit of knowledge eventually ruins them. Unlike the heroes of Mary Shelley and Robert Louis Stevenson, however, the passion for knowledge evidenced by Doyle's hero does not lead to his death. M'Vittie becomes a better scientist because he now appreciates the strength of human attachment and understands science's obligation to serve human needs. In fact, it is love that saves M'Vittie. The lonely researcher's loathing for his fellow creatures, another kind of passion which might have destroyed him, has been mitigated by his experience of the love of Ourganeff and Sophie. "I sometimes have thought that their spirits, flit like shadowy sea birds, move over the wild waters of the bay" (*Polestar,* 141).

In this way "The Man from Archangel" represents something of a turning point in Doyle's career. Out of his stories about passion has evolved M'Vittie, a man whose passion is yoked to the service of science. When "The Man from Archangel" resolves itself in a kind of qualified approval of the life lived in the impassioned service of the intellect, it points the way to Doyle's most famous exemplar of that life, the master detective Sherlock Holmes.

Doyle's tales of terror show that there are things that cannot be known, or can only be half-known, and that these secrets are dangerous to us. In their qualified resolutions, these tales seem to suggest the need for another form, one in which these uncertainties can be faced squarely and in which mysteries are solvable and secrets understood. Doyle found this form in the detective story and in the invention of a character, the detective, who would make a practical and social application of the knowledge that the scientist pursued in lonely experimentation. Through a combination of induction and deduction, the scientist and the detective solve the mysteries with which they are faced. But while the scientist, alone in his remote laboratory, runs the risk of wasting his life in pursuit of sterile knowledge, the detective brings that knowledge into the realm of the social. In so doing he is charged with protecting the truth and undertakes, as the editors of a recent collection of essays on detective fiction point out, "the full facing of criminality, even horror, and all its implications."[21]

In turning M'Vittie back from the pursuit of sterile knowledge by humanizing his research, Doyle marked the beginning of his turn toward a character whose scientific pursuits would have social application. In 1886, the year after the publication of "The Man from Archangel," he took the next step toward alleviating the Gothic pattern of failure and death into which his characters had been locked. He decided to write a story using a scientist in a structure that assumes that the solution to mysteries can be found. The horror story which, as Dorothy Sayers says, "must always leave us guessing" was to be replaced by the detective story which "seeks to leave nothing unexplained."[22] The ambiguous M'Vittie was to be overshadowed by the heroic Holmes.

Chapter Three

The Beginnings of a Modern Hero: Sherlock Holmes

Although greatly pleased with the success of his stories of mystery and adventure, by the end of 1885 Doyle felt "capable" as he reports in his autobiography "of something fresher and crisper and more workmanlike" (*MA*, 69). That same year had seen him produce his first full-length novel, *The Firm of Girdlestone,* a book which was a great disappointment to the author because he felt then, and later, that it was badly written and, "like the first book of everyone else . . . too reminiscent of the work of others" (*MA*, 69).

Fresh from what he saw as a failure, Doyle determined to write another book because, as he explained, "I could go on doing short stories forever and never make headway. What is necessary is that your name should be on the back of a volume" (*MA*, 68). Since Edgar Allan Poe's detective, Monsieur Dupin, "had from boyhood been one of my heroes," and the "neat dovetailing" of Emile Gaboriau's plots had always pleased him, Doyle decided to write a full-length detective story.

After some hesitation about names (his original choice of the Irish name Sherringford was soon changed to Sherlock), the novelist assembled what he called his "puppets," Dr. Watson and Mr. Holmes, and wrote *A Study in Scarlet* (1887). In later years, when Sherlock Holmes had become one of the most famous fictional protagonists of his day, Doyle claimed that the character of the detective was largely inspired by his recollections of one of his medical school teachers, Dr. Joseph Bell. Dr. Bell's famous exhortations to the students to use their inductive and deductive powers before making a diagnosis was no doubt a factor in Doyle's creation of Holmes, but the character's literary antecedents, the detectives created by Eugene Vidocq, Edgar Allan Poe, Emile Gaboriau, Charles Dickens, and Wilkie Collins, are clearly the true sources for Holmes.

Poe and Gaboriau

Edgar Allan Poe's creation, Monsieur Dupin, was a sophisticated, highly educated man, quite capable of discussing science or the classics with equal facility. In the "Murders in the Rue Morgue" Dupin's superior intellect is demonstrated on the first page, when he correctly deduces his friend's thoughts. His scientific ability is demonstrated when, after observing some strands of hair left clutched in a dead woman's hand, Dupin gives his friend a book and tells him to make note of "a minute anatomical and generally descriptive account of the large fulvous Ourang-Outang of the East Indian Islands."[1] And later on in "The Mystery of Marie Roget" (1842) Dupin discourses on various scientific subjects, including the nature of fungi and the rate at which grass grows. This academic act, which substantiates Dupin's own scientific knowledge "by reference to a text-book which the detective is able to take from his own book-shelves,"[2] was to become a standard part of detective fiction that featured gentleman detectives. Certainly, Doyle was not averse to using this scene to substantiate Holmes's astuteness.

With his Dupin stories, Poe set a pattern for detective fiction that was to dominate the genre. Not only do the plots of his tales include most of the devices still used by writers of detective fiction, but, for the first time, the reader was expected to think analytically and to follow the logical arguments made by the detective.

The young French writer Emile Gaboriau read Poe's stories and was so "filled with admiration"[3] for them that he created a gentleman detective of his own. Monsieur Lecoq was introduced to the public in a series of full-length novels published in France in the 1860s. Gaboriau is largely responsible for the form known as the *roman policier* or police story because Lecoq is a public defender of law and order employed by the police department. While Poe's Dupin is a private detective who works solely for his own amusement and can, in true gentlemanly fashion, often solve the case from his armchair, the official Lecoq, in contrast, is much more energetic and throws himself into the case with intense physical as well as mental activity.

In Doyle's development of the genre these separate aspects of the detective were to be combined into the character of the zealous gentleman detective, Sherlock Holmes. According to the nature of the case, and his own mood, Holmes can be mentally active, like Dupin, while lounging in his flat, or physically and mentally active, like Lecoq, at the scene of the crime. In one important respect, though, all the detectives are similar, for as one recent critic concludes, they all "regard a mysterious puzzle as a challenge to their powers of perception: they reason with mathematical precision and enjoy giving little lectures to their associates."[4]

Dupin, Lecoq, and the later creations of Charles Dickens and Wilkie Collins were all to stand Doyle in good stead, for those earlier writers firmly planted the idea of the detective as a hero in the reading public's consciousness. In 1886, making full use of the possibilities that other detective writers had already suggested, Doyle returned to Poe's idea of the individualistic gentleman detective to create his own character, "a stereotype of the private detective as complete and expressive of its time" as any of the earlier creations had been.[5]

A *Study in Scarlet*

Although Holmes was to become one of the most famous characters in British literature, the book that introduces him was not initially a success. Doyle first sent the manuscript of *A Study In Scarlet* to his friend and mentor James Payn of the *Cornhill*. Payn rejected it because it was, he said, too long for a short story and too short for a serial. By the end of the summer of 1886 *A Study In Scarlet* had been rejected, unread, by two other publishers.

Doyle was beginning to despair of ever having his story read, much less published, when Ward, Lock and Co. offered, rather tentatively, in October 1886 to put the work in their 1887 Christmas annual if the author would accept twenty-five pounds for the entire copyright. Reluctantly, because he would have to wait eighteen months for publication and because he had hoped for an offer based on royalties, Doyle accepted their proposal. *A Study in Scarlet* was finally published in *Beeton's Christmas Annual* for 1887 to very little critical attention. Indeed, it is doubtful if any of the influential critics even knew of the story's existence. Despite what Doyle describes as "some little favorable comment" (*MA,* 71), *A Study in Scarlet* was neither a critical nor a popular success. Ward, Lock and Co. did sell out their Christmas annual and did reissue Doyle's novel under separate cover early in the following year, but to all intents and purposes Holmes was dead.[6]

Doyle was very discouraged by the early death of his detective novel. He liked the story well enough, but his main concern was not for the story; it was for his own lack of literary recognition. The door to literary success, as he notes in his autobiography, "still seemed to be barred" (*MA*, 71). It was not until almost two years later that an American editor, who had read and liked *A Study in Scarlet*, approached Doyle and commissioned him to write another book about Sherlock Holmes for immediate publication in *Lippincott's* magazine. Doyle quickly resurrected the detective, and *The Sign of Four* appeared in *Lippincott's* in February 1890.

A Study in Scarlet begins by introducing the reader and Dr. John Watson to a reclusive scientist. Holmes is first described by a mutual acquaintance, Stamford, as "a little queer in his ideas, an enthusiast in some branches of science."[7] Stamford goes on to say that although Holmes's studies are "desultory and eccentric" and that the scientist seems to have no plans to use his knowledge, Holmes is "well up in anatomy and is a first class chemist."

Stamford's description is borne out when he and Watson actually go to meet Holmes in the laboratory where he is working. Watson reports that "there was only one student in the room, who was bending over a table absorbed in his work." When the student heard them, "he sprang to his feet with a cry of pleasure. 'I've found it! I've found it,' he shouted to my companion running towards us with a test-tube in his hand. 'I have found a re-agent which is precipitated by hemoglobin, and by nothing else.' Had he discovered a gold mine, greater delight could not have shown upon his features" (*CH*, 1:17).

When Watson fails to understand the practical effects of Holmes's discovery, the scientist educates him: "It is the most practical medico-legal discovery for years. Don't you see that it gives us an infallible test for bloodstains?" (*CH*, 1:14). Holmes's enthusiasm for applied science is emphasized throughout this scene and again in a similar scene in *The Sign of Four*, when Holmes employs the time he must spend waiting for information on the Sholto case in "abstruse chemical analysis" which continues "up to the small hours of the morning." (*CH*, 1:130)

In spite of Holmes's commitment to science, he is not the complete man of science that some later detectives, for example Arthur Morrison's Dr. Thorndyke, would be. Holmes is a keen student of those areas of science that, by adding to his practical knowledge, will help solve cases, but he is not a theoretical scientist. His devotion to applied science is vividly expressed by Stamford, who comments, "I could imagine his giving a friend a little pinch of the latest vegetable alkaloid, not out of malevolence, you understand, but simply out of a spirit of inquiry in order to have a more accurate idea of its effects" (*CH*, 1:17). But Holmes's antipathy to theoretical scientific knowledge is emphasized by his curt rejoinder to Watson's surprise when he discovers that Holmes knows nothing of the Copernican theory. " 'But the Solar System!' I protested. 'What the deuce is it to me?' he interrupted impatiently, 'you say that we go round the sun. If we went round the moon it would not make a pennyworth of difference to me or to my work' " (*CH*, 1:21).

This last quote is particularly informative. The science that interests Holmes is of the kind that will help him do his "work." The most attractive aspect of Holmes as a scientist is that he can use just as much or as little scientific knowledge as he needs in order to solve society's puzzles. Science is an aid to Holmes; it is not an end in itself. This attitude also serves to emphasize his sense of control. Holmes's success as the only private "consulting detective" (*CH*, 1:24) depends not on the depth of his scientific knowledge, but rather on his perception of what is or is not necessary, a trait that demonstrates his ability to make sense of the world.

Above all, Holmes is a rationalist, and it is as a rationalist that he solves the mystery of his first case. The adventure of *A Study in Scarlet* begins with a message summoning Holmes to number 3, Lauriston Gardens. Holmes and Watson hurry off to this address where the police show them the body of a dead man lying in the middle of an empty room, which has the word *Rache* scrawled in blood on one wall. As Holmes leaves the scene of the crime, the baffled police, who think that the word may be the first part of a woman's name, are enlightened when the detective tells them that the word is German for "revenge." The case does indeed turn out to be one of revenge, for the dead man, Enoch Drebber, was a Mormon, whose efforts many years earlier to marry a young girl against her will had led to her suicide. The girl's former fiancée, Ferrier, who had dedicated his life to wreaking revenge on her persecutors, had accomplished his aim with the murder of Enoch Drebber and his secretary, Joseph Stangerson.

The first half of the novel, a traditional detective story complete with clues, a search for further information, and a denouement in which Holmes unmasks the killer, is concerned with the identity of the murderer of Enoch Drebber. The second half of the story, told as a separate adventure story complete with a faraway place, hero, heroine, and band of murderous villains, concerns itself with the motive of the crime. Doyle had not yet solved one of the technical difficulties of the detective formula: how to explain the events that led up to the murder without breaking what one critic calls the "thread of the detective interest."[8]

Doyle did not yet know how to do that, therefore the interest in the detective in this story *is* broken. The two parts of *A Study in Scarlet* are completely different from each other. The American adventure story, set in the arid, sunbaked plains of Utah, is juxtaposed to the English detective story, set in gaslit, foggy London, without any viable transition. By using two such different locations, Doyle had to write two separate stories, a position that left him with a badly split narrative. The modern reader, however, is usually willing to overlook the flawed structure of this story and affectionately remember Holmes's part of the novel not only because it contains all the excitement and charm of the world of 221B Baker Street but also because it is the story that first introduced us to Sherlock Holmes.

The Sign of Four

By the time Doyle came to write his second full-length Holmes story, *The Sign of Four* (1890), published in America as *The Sign of the Four,* he had learned how to avoid the same narrative mistake. Instead of dividing the novel into two radically discrete segments dealing with a crime and its long-hidden motive, the mystery and its solution are unraveled in a more or less organic fashion, with information about past events integrated gradually into the action to provide both motive and explanation.

For Holmes and Watson, the adventure begins with the arrival of Mary Morstan, who tells them that every year since the disappearance of her father ten years before, she has received a perfect pearl sent through the mail. This year, however, she has received a letter asking her to go to a rendezvous that night and to bring two friends with her. Watson, Holmes, and Mary go all together to the meeting that takes place in a strange house outside London owned by Mr. Thaddeus Sholto. Thaddeus is the son of a great friend of Mary's father, a man who, Thaddeus explains, has deprived

Mary of her rightful share of a treasure that their fathers had stolen during the Indian mutiny.

The treasure is hidden at Pondicherry Lodge, at the home of Thaddeus's twin brother, Bartholemew, but when they get there, they find only the body of the mysteriously murdered Bartholemew. The bungling police (led by Mr. Athelney Jones) arrest Thaddeus for the murder of his brother, leaving Holmes to solve the triple mysteries of who got into the locked and barred room, how Sholto was killed, and the location of the lost treasure. From various pieces of evidence found in the room, Holmes deduces that the murdering intruders were a man with a wooden leg and a small human being approximately the size of a child. Recognizing a dartlike wound in the neck of the victim, Holmes decides that the "child" is in fact an aborigine of the Andaman Islands.

This supposition is later validated by a book that Holmes, like Dupin, pulls off his bookshelf and gives to Watson to read. Watson finds out that the native inhabitants of these islands situated in the Bay of Bengal are "naturally hideous, having large mis-shapen heads, small fierce eyes and distorted features" (*CH,* 1:128). Further evidence of Holmes's brilliance is provided when the description continues with the information that the aborigines are cannibals who kill their victims with poisoned arrows shot from blowpipes. The little simian creature in this case turns out to be the devoted slave of one Jonathan Small, another accomplice in the Indian looting affair, who has now returned with his companion to steal the treasure. After an exciting nighttime riverboat chase, Holmes and Watson capture Small but, in a gesture intriguing for its implications as to the value of native life, they hill the hideous Tonga.

Many critics have noted the similarity between *The Sign of Four* and Poe's story "The Murders in the Rue Morgue." While there are obvious connections (for example, the scene in which Holmes examines the locked room resembles Dupin's examination of the bloodstained room in the Rue Morgue, and the subhuman Tonga, who knows nothing of Western morality is an approximation of Poe's orangutan, who kills only when he is afraid), *The Sign of Four* is a more complex and interesting working out of Poe's story.

The relationship between Holmes and Watson develops complexities that go far beyond the simple speaker-interlocutor relationship of Dupin and his friend. *The Sign of Four* begins with Holmes reaching for the cocaine bottle—"I find it so transcendently

stimulating," he explains (*CH*, 1:89)—and with Watson's indignant paternal response to his friend's habit: "Count the Cost! Your
brain may, as you say, be roused and excited but it is a pathological
and morbid process which involves increased tissue-change and may
at least leave a permanent weakness. . . . Remember that I speak
not only as one comrade to another but as a medical man to one
for whose constitution he is to some extent answerable" (*CH*, 1:89).
Watson's assumption of responsibility for Holmes's well-being is
an indication of the rapid development of his affection for his fellow
lodger.

Later on in the same scene, the reader learns that the antisocial
Holmes reciprocates the feeling. Testing his deductive powers on
Watson's watch, a common object which, Holmes explains, has
"the impress of individuality upon it in such a way that a trained
observer might read it" (*CH*, 1:92), Holmes proclaims that it was
once the property of a weak man who eventually became a drunkard.
Yet when Holmes learns that he has accurately described the doctor's
brother, he realizes that his observations may have hurt Watson and
he is moved to generous solicitude for his friend. " 'My dear doctor,'
said he kindly, 'pray accept my apologies. Viewing the matter as
an abstract problem, I had forgotten how personal and painful a
thing it might be to you' " (*CH*, 1:93).

The Sign of Four pictures Holmes and Watson as trusty friends
and comrades in arms whose domestic life is well established. Indeed, the affection that exists between them is based on and nour-
ished by their domestic life together. At the beginning of the story,
in an opening that was to become a tradition in the Holmes stories,
the detective is between cases. Watson and Holmes lounge around
their cosy flat, the one a victim of "my wounded leg which ached
wearily at every change of the weather" and the other a victim of
"the dull routine of existence" (*CH*, 1:90). The flat at 221B Baker
Street provides them with a haven from the world outside. Like
their world, it is comfortable and masculine, a place to be free from
women and from emotional attachments to the opposite sex. The
only woman who has a right to penetrate its recesses is Mrs. Hudson,
whose function as housekeeper is to prepare wonderful meals, to
straighten up the mess in the sitting room, and to show visitors in
and out. The two men, who behave as if they had always lived
together, smoke, read, eat, and carry on a conversation in a setting
reminiscent of the best men's clubs.

Miss Mary Morstan's appeal for help jolts the friends out of their everyday routine and out of their comfortable world. "The adventure," as one critic has pointed out, "is always and everywhere a passage between the known and the unknown."[9] In *The Sign of Four*, as well as later stories, the known is a warm, safe, brightly lit set of rooms, and the unknown is the cold, dark, dangerous city of London. Whenever Watson and Holmes leave their snug flat, they must venture into an outside world that demonstrates, in no uncertain meteorogical terms, the extent of the dangers that face them. As they accompany Miss Morstan, Watson describes the city. "It was a September evening and not yet seven o'clock but the day had been a dreary one and a dense drizzly fog lay low upon the great city. Mud-colored clouds drooped sadly over the muddy streets. Down the street the lamps were but misty splotches of diffused light which threw a feeble circular glimmer upon the slimy pavement. The yellow glare from the shop-windows streamed out into the steamy vaporous air and threw a murky, shifting radiance across the crowded thoughfare" (*CH,* 1:151).

The imagery in this passage is typical of all the Holmes stories. The unknown, the place where the crimes are committed and the place to which the friends must venture is usually dark and wet. Doyle consistently uses words like "dreary," "dense," "murky," "eerie," "misty," and "vaporous" to describe the conditions where the adventures start. So pervasive is this idea that the passage quoted above can be found, with some slight modifications, in all of the Holmes stories. The outside world of adventure, where Holmes quite literally goes forth into the darkness, is characterized by bad weather, and the inside world of domesticity is always characterized by physical comfort. Doyle continually juxtaposes warm-cold, dry-wet, and light-dark imagery to emphasize the differences between the known and the unknown in Holmes's world.

As the hero of this journey, Holmes is not bothered by the dark, the fog, or the rain, for he alone can, as Watson tells us, "rise superior to petty influences" (*CH,* 1:99). In a Gothic story where nature exactly reflects the hero's internal world, the onset of a storm often presages a turning point in the protagonist's condition. In detective fiction the weather, reflecting the state of the external world, measures the detective's ability to control that world insofar as he is not affected by atmospheric conditions. Watson and Miss Morstan are both made nervous and depressed by the drizzly fog, but Holmes —as always—is oblivious to the foul weather. If Holmes can deal with the rain, then presumably he can deal with the forces of evil that are made manifest in the weather.

As the hero, Holmes must also be able to penetrate the darkness. When they are in a cab, Holmes takes out a "pocket-lantern" so that he can continue to note down various "figures and memoranda" (*CH*, 1:99). Later on when they are shut up in another cab, darkened in a deliberate attempt to hide the direction of their journey, Holmes, unable to see but by no means made helpless, "muttered the names [of the streets] as the cab rattled through squares and in and out by tortuous by-streets" (*CH*, 1:99). Again, when they are involved in the river chase at night, Holmes pulls out his "night-glasses" which enable him to see to the opposite shore.

The extraordinary powers Holmes displays enable him to dominate another register of experience in these stories—that of the supernatural. There are numerous incidents in *A Study in Scarlet* and *The Sign of Four* that hint at the possibility of the involvement of a supernatural agency. John Rance is murdered in a room splattered with blood that is not his; Bartholomew Sholto is dispatched in a locked and barred room. But Holmes is so thoroughly rational that he will not countenance any explanation for these events that is not "natural." As the arch-rationalist explains to a credulous Watson in the case of "The Sussex Vampire": "Are we to give serious attention to such things? This agency stands flat-footed upon the ground, and there it must remain. The world is big enough for us. No ghosts need apply" (*CH*, 2:1034). His struggles are with human beings whose actions, often bizarre and frequently evil, can always be explained. The forces that lurk in the dark on the edge of the darkness and fogs of London are often terrifying, but they are never, in a Sherlock Holmes story, the product of supernatural agents.

Although it is often neglected as one of the early Holmes tales, *The Sign of Four* contains some of Doyle's most powerful writing. Notable is the final chase scene on the river Thames, where Watson, Holmes, and the police, confined to a launch, try to overtake Small and his aborigine companion in a charted boat that goes "like the devil" (*CH*, 1:137). The sun has sunk and it is now dark as the two boats speed down the river: "Our boilers were strained to their utmost, and the frail shell vibrated and creaked with the fierce energy which was driving us along . . . Jones turned our searchlight upon her, so that we could plainly see the figures upon her deck

. . . The boy held the tiller, while against the red glare of the furnace I could see old Smith, stripped to the waist and shovelling coals for dear life" (*CH,* 1:138).

This Inferno-like description, which has the fervid quality of a nightmare, is the backdrop for the evil embodied in the subhuman Tonga. The "unhallowed dwarf" is first seen as "a dark mass which looked like a Newfoundland dog" (*CH,* 1:138) lying quietly in the bottom of the boat. As their launch approached the *Aurora* and Small is threatened with capture, the mass ominously comes alive: "There was movement in the huddled bundle upon the deck. It straightened itself into a little black man . . . with a great misshapen head and a shock of tangled, dishevelled hair . . . Never have I seen features so deeply marked with bestiality and cruelty. His small eyes glowed and burned with a sombre light, and his thick lips were writhed back from his teeth which grinned and chattered at us with half-animal fury" (*CH,* 1:138).

In what was to be a rare example of Holmes and Watson dispensing justice, the friends shoot Tonga just as he fires his poisoned dart at them. "Our pistols rang out together. He whirled around, threw up his arms, and, with a kind of choking cough, fell sideways into the stream. I caught one glimpse of his venomous, menacing eyes amid the white swirl of the water" (*CH,* 1:139). The mastermind of the affair, Jonathan Small, is captured and handed over to the police, but the animalistic Tonga, a creature well outside the boundaries of any expectation of rational behavior, is shot.

The ending of *The Sign of Four* seems to signal the end of the Watson/Holmes partnership. The masculine domesticity of Baker Street is to be replaced, Watson tells Holmes, by the more usual kind: "I feel that it may be the last investigation in which I shall have the chance of studying your methods. Miss Morstan has done me the honor to accept me as a husband in prospective" (*CH,* 1:157). Watson is to take the expected path of love and marriage, while the solitary Holmes returns to the hypodermic syringe: " 'For me' said Sherlock Holmes, 'there still remains the cocaine-bottle' " (*CH,* 1:158).

The division of interests here is an important one, for it shows the price that the detective must pay for his extraordinary powers. To have the necessary authority, to be capable of bringing order to the chaos of modern life, Holmes must subordinate all emotion to the service of the intellect. Holmes has the kind of single-minded obsessional focus that Doyle's earlier Gothic characters had, but, because the detective's world is one that is susceptible to a rational ordering, Holmes's obsession has to remain free of emotion. As Holmes succinctly puts it, "But love is an emotional thing, and whatever is emotional is opposed to that true cold reason which I place above all things. I should never marry myself, lest I bias my judgment" (CH, 1:157).

Fortunately, Watson's decision to give up his partnership with Holmes was only a temporary one. When Doyle began to write the later series of short stories about Holmes, he needed Watson to chronicle the adventures, so Watson's marriage (or as some students of these works claim, marriages) recedes into the background. On some occasions it appears that Watson's wife has died, and on others that she has simply gone to visit her mother, but whatever the excuse given, the purpose is clear: Watson must be free to keep Holmes company and to narrate the story.

Therefore, in spite of his marriage(s), Baker Street is still home for Watson, and he continues to return. Indeed in the first of the short stories, "A Scandal in Bohemia," Watson "accidentally" finds himself outside 221B, where he is "seized with a keen desire to see Holmes again and to know how he was employing his extraordinary powers." (CH, 1:161) Watson's involvement is clinched when he sees through the window that Holmes is "at work again." Watson cannot stay away; he rings the bell, goes up to what he lovingly calls "the old room," and the next adventure begins.

The Sign of Four was produced in London in volume form in the spring of 1890, while at the same time *A Study in Scarlet* was published in the United States as a dime novel. Both novels, immediately popular in the United States, were less enthusiastically greeted by the British public. The author himself was not even very interested in these novels. One of his biographers who has had access to Doyle's private papers notes: "he made not a single contemporary reference to *The Sign of Four* in letter, notebook, or diary."[10] Doyle, busy writing his second historical novel, *The White Company,* was far too absorbed in what he called "the most complete, satisfying and ambitious work that I have ever done" (MA, 75) to worry about "two little books" (MA, 90).

However, in spite of the relative success of his work, Doyle was still troubled by financial matters, so he thought of sending two new Holmes stories to a recently published magazine called the

Strand. Commenting on his idea, Doyle says: "it had struck me that a single character running through a series, if it only engaged the attention of the reader, would bind that reader to that particular magazine . . . Clearly the ideal compromise was a character which carried through, and yet installments which were complete in themselves . . . I believe that I was the first to realise this and *'The Strand Magazine'* the first to put it into practice" (*MA,* 90). The editor of the *Strand,* Greenhough Smith, bought the first two stories and immediately commissioned four more. The first of the series of six, "A Scandal in Bohemia" appeared in the July 1891 issue, whereupon Sherlock Holmes and Conan Doyle were famous overnight.

The Adventures of Sherlock Holmes

After the first six stories ("A Scandal in Bohemia," "The Red-Headed League," "A Case of Identity," "The Boscombe Valley Mystery," "The Five Orange Pips," and "The Man With The Twisted Lip"), Doyle was to call the rest of the Holmes stories ("The Adventure of the Blue Carbuncle," "The Speckled Band," "The Engineer's Thumb," "The Noble Bachelor," "The Beryl Coronet," and "The Adventure of the Copper Beaches") "adventures" and his choice of words not only tells something about the form of the stories, but also suggests why they were so popular. Joseph Campbell maintains that the need to experience vicariously the trials and rewards of an adventure is common to all people and every culture; "the one shape-shifting yet marvelously constant story that we find, together with a challengingly persistent suggestion of more remaining to be experienced than will ever be known or told."[11] While this critic places emphasis on the central formula of the story remaining the same—the hero undertakes the adventure, passes the trials, and finally returns to society bearing the prize that is both reward and witness to his participation—this observation becomes more telling when we recognize that the characteristics of the hero do change to reflect the concerns and anxieties of their historical moment.

Unlike the mythological heroes who are lured, carried, or in some way mystically summoned to undertake the quest, Holmes is prosaically introduced to his adventure by a person, a letter, a telegram, or even an article in the newspaper. The physical trials that beset the hero have been translated, in the Holmes stories, into the mental trial that is the continuous sifting of the mass of information that surrounds the case. Holmes is aided in his travels to search out the truth, not by any magical helpers, like small animals, gnomes, or witches, but by trains that run on time, by hansom cabs that appear whenever they are needed, and by newspapers that publish advertisements instantaneously. When Holmes returns from the place of trial, the murky, rain-sodden, gray city, he brings back with him the traditional "boon," the restoration of order.

However, unlike the traditional mythic gift of order, this restoration is only temporary. Holmes's London is too dangerous and too evil to be permanently settled. The mystery is solved, the criminal is apprehended, and, for that moment at least, order has been brought out of chaos. Doyle has maintained the central formula of the adventure story, while creating a heroic figure who is uniquely capable of dealing with the mysteries of his own time. Recently described as "a cliché whose time had come,"[12] Holmes can be seen, in the general acclaim that greeted all the stories, to be the perfect hero for late Victorian England.

The perfect hero of the stories was not quite the same character who had appeared in the novels, however, nor was the world that he inhabited quite the same world. The original series of six stories, appearing in the *Strand* between July 1891 and June 1892, portray a Holmes who is becoming more conventional and middle-class. For example, the detective's cocaine habit is barely mentioned in the stories. There is one passing reference to his practice in "A Scandal in Bohemia," but Holmes is never again seen actually reaching for the syringe. The irascible, patently antisocial character gives way to a softer, more courteous person, one not so prone to the moody silences of the earlier works. Holmes now begins and ends his cases with a long conversation with Watson and, when the case is completed, instead of retreating into solitude, Holmes is more likely to suggest an evening on the town.

The kinds of crimes with which the stories are concerned further underscore this difference. The garish murders of the first two novels are largely replaced with mysteries, less grim and more ordinary. "A Scandal in Bohemia" concerns the possible blackmailing of the king of Bohemia by his former mistress, Irene Adler, a woman who so impresses Holmes with her courage and daring that he was afterwards always to refer to her, Watson tells us, "under the honourable title of *the* woman" (*CH,* 1:161). When Irene Adler falls in love and marries "a better man" (*CH,* 1:179), the blackmailing never takes place, so no crime is committed.

The mystery in "The Red-Headed League" concerns the hiring of a red-headed man to copy entries from the *Encyclopaedia Britannica.* Holmes discovers that the objective of this strange employment is to remove Mr. Wilson from his pawnbroker business because the bank adjacent to Mr. Wilson's shop is being tunneled into by a gang of thieves. Holmes seizes the robbers before they can carry out their robbery.

"A Case of Identity," the third story, has to do with a stepfather's plan to maintain control of his daughter's independent income. In order to do this, the stepfather, Mr. Windibank, impersonates a younger man, known as Hosmer Angel, so that his stepdaughter, Mary Sutherland, will fall in love with Mr. Angel, not marry anyone else, and not take her money out of the family. On their wedding day, however, the husband-to-be disappears, never to be heard of again. This mystery, brought to Holmes by Miss Sutherland, is solved when the detective proves Mr. Windibank and Mr. Angel are one and the same by comparing two separate typewritten notes which show, by a disfigurement in the letters, that they were typed on the same machine.

The next two stories, "The Boscombe Valley Mystery" and "The Five Orange Pips," revert to Doyle's original formula. Both deal with unexplained murders, and both are ultimately discovered to be revenge murders. The final story of the first series of six, "The Man With the Twisted Lip," is again concerned with a question of impersonation and is again a story in which no crime has been committed. Mr. Neville St. Clair, a prosperous, happily married man, has disappeared under suspicious circumstances. His wife, unexpectedly in London for the day, actually sees him in a top window as she makes her way through an alley in the disreputable East End of London. She rushes up to the room, but he is gone, although his clothes are there, and in his place is a wounded beggar man who claims never to have known or seen St. Clair. The police arrest the beggar for the murder of St. Clair and put him in prison. After one or two false starts, Holmes realizes that the beggar man must be St. Clair himself and proves it by washing off the beggar's makeup while he is asleep in his cell. St. Clair explains that he can make more money by begging than by his former work as a journalist, but in lieu of any punishment, he promises Holmes that he will not beg again. St. Clair is reunited with his wife and children while Holmes and Watson go off happily to have breakfast together.

The change in the nature of the mysteries that Holmes is asked to solve does not go unnoticed even by the detective himself. In "The Blue Carbuncle," the first story of the second series of six published in the *Strand* between June and December 1892, Holmes explains the difference to Watson. The doctor opines that a hat that Holmes is holding probably has some "deadly story" (*CH*, 1:245) associated with it: " 'No crime,' says Sherlock Holmes, laughing. 'Only one of those whimsical little incidents which will happen when you have four million human beings all jostling each other within the space of a few square miles. Amid the action and reaction of so dense a swarm of humanity, every possible combination of events may be expected to take place, and many a little problem will be presented which may be striking and bizarre without being criminal' " (*CH*, 1:245).

Holmes's role as a problem solver of the "little incidents" of urban life gives him a new position as a moral judge of humanity. When a crime has been committed, he turns the guilty party over to the police. In cases where no crime has been committed, Holmes is the fatherly judge who pronounces a future course of behavior for the transgressor. Mr. Holder, who has wrongfully accused his son, Arthur, of stealing a valuable coronet in the eleventh story, "The Adventure of the Beryl Coronet," is told by Holmes what to do to make up for his accusation: "You owe a very humble apology to that noble lad, your son, who has carried himself in this matter as I should be proud to see my own son, should I ever have chance to have one" (*CH*, 1:313). "The Adventure of the Noble Bachelor" similarly concludes when Holmes, finding the missing couple, Mr. and Mrs. Moulton, tells us, "I ventured to give them some paternal advice and to point out to them that it would be better in every way that they should make their position a little clearer" (*CH*, 1:300).

Holmes's position as a moral arbitrator sometimes extends further than the giving of advice. In "A Case of Identity" Mr. Windibank has committed no crime for which he can be charged. However, he has, Holmes says, played "as cruel, and selfish and heartless a trick in a petty way as ever came before me" (*CH*, 1:200). When Mr. Windibank sneers at this description, the detective decides to administer his own brand of justice; "It is not part of my duties to my client, but here's a hunting crop handy, and I think I shall just treat myself to . . ." (*CH*, 1:201). Unfortunately the villain rushes off before Holmes can thrash him, but the detective's willingness to undertake this act emphasizes his position as the enforcer of standards of decency in cases that are not covered by the civil or criminal code.

Finally, Holmes's physical appearance is also altered during his tenure in the stories. Doyle's description of the Holmes that he had originally conceived is not prepossessing; "He [Holmes] had, as I imagined him, a thin razor-like face, with a great hawks-bill of a nose, and two small eyes, set close together on either side of it" (*MA*, 101). However, Sidney Paget's illustrations, which had been commissioned by the *Strand* for Doyle's stories, gave Doyle's readers a different idea of Holmes. Paget's Holmes is elegant, slim, and handsome, with an aristocratic profile, hooded eyes, and long thin sensitive hands. Although this version of Holmes was not similar to Doyle's idea, the writer apparently gave his tacit consent to Paget's version; "It chanced, however," he explains, "that poor Sidney Paget, who, before his premature death drew all the original pictures, had a younger brother whose name, I think, was Walter, who served him as a model. The handsome Walter took the place of the uglier Sherlock, and perhaps from the point of view of my lady readers it was as well" (*MA*, 101).

Doyle's original commission had been for six stories and that is all he intended to write. In October 1891, he was about to begin a new historical novel (tentatively called *The Refugees*) he was waiting for *The White Company* to appear, and, as he says," I was weary . . . of inventing plots" (*MA*, 92). He was tired of the narrative demands that short stories imposed on him, but, as the editors of the *Strand* and the magazine's many readers were begging him to write more detective stories, he decided to let the publishers and editors of the magazine decide. He asked for what he considered to be an outrageously high price for each story, fifty pounds, and then he added the condition, "irrespective of length."[13] To his surprise and dismay, Greenhough Smith accepted these terms by return post.

Determined that the Holmes stories should not keep him from work that was "more ambitious from a literary point of view" (*MA*, 92), Doyle sat down and wrote "The Adventure of the Blue Carbuncle" and "The Adventure of the Speckled Band" in one week.

Two weeks later, when he had completed all but one of the promised six, he was still chafing at the strictures on his time. So, before he wrote the last of the twelve, "The Adventure of the Copper Beeches," he suggested in a letter to his mother that he would kill Holmes off.[14] But Mrs. Doyle, or "the Ma'am" as she was always known, was one of Holmes's greatest fans and, on this occasion at least, she managed to dissuade her son.

Holmes was still alive, but Doyle had no intention of using him again. By February 1892, however, the *Strand* magazine had badgered him for more Holmes material to such an extent that again he made them an offer that he was sure they would refuse. This time he asked for one thousand pounds for a dozen stories with the attendant condition that he would not write them immediately or indeed to any fixed schedule. And once again much to Doyle's chagrin, the *Strand* accepted his terms without question or delay.

Doyle had won a respite, not a reprieve, from "the heartless calculating-machine"[15] that the Holmes stories had become for him. He wrote "Silver Blaze," "The Cardboard Box," and "The Yellow Face" during 1892, leaving the bulk of the remaining twelve stories to be written early in 1893 while he was in Switzerland, where he had taken Touie for her health. By the time he reached Davos, Doyle was very tired of Holmes and Watson and the complicated plots they required; "the difficulty of the Holmes work," Doyle complained, "was that every story really needed as clear-cut and original a plot as a longish book would do. One cannot without effort spin plots at such a rate. They are apt to become thin and break" (*MA*, 91–92).

Ever since he had made the suggestion to his mother some fourteen months earlier, he had continued to entertain the idea of killing Holmes. And when, as part of a one-day Swiss excursion, he took Touie to visit the Reichenbach Falls, he found the sight personally terrifying, yet literally useful because he knew they "would make a worthy tomb for poor Sherlock, even if I buried my bank account along with him" (*MA*, 93–94). In April 1893 he wrote what he believed to be the last Holmes story, "The Final Problem" (published December 1893). To the public's great dismay, and to Doyle's great relief, Holmes saved the world from the arch-villain Dr. Moriarty, although in doing so he lost his life at the Reichenbach Falls.

In retrospect, it is hard to understand the depth of Doyle's dislike of his creation. The Holmes adventures had relieved him of all his financial worries. The fame of Holmes and Watson had made the name of Arthur Conan Doyle a household word. Probably the fact of the matter is that Holmes was too popular; not only did he intrude into Doyle's private life, when, for instance, the mail addressed to Holmes was delivered to Doyle, but he overshadowed the historical romances, the work that Doyle considered his best. Speaking of his decision to kill off Holmes, Doyle said, "At last, after I had done two series of them [the adventures], I saw that I was in danger of having my hand forced, and of being entirely identified with what I regarded as a lower stratum of literary achievement" (*MA, 93*).

The higher stratum that Doyle aspired to could be found in his historical romances, but the public's infatuation with Holmes prevented his more serious work from getting either the popular or critical attention that it deserved. Doyle wanted to be known as an important writer. And the Sherlock Holmes stories were not, he felt, serious fiction. He also feared that the easy success and huge sums of money might corrupt him to such an extent that one day he would find himself unable to do without either. For all these reasons then, Doyle heartily disliked Holmes and Watson. It was with a great sigh of relief that he turned his back on the public's demands that he somehow write more stories featuring their favorite character; deaf to each and every demand, he turned to his "honest" work, the historical novels.

Chapter Four
The Most Important Work: Seven Historical Novels

Micah Clarke (1889), the first of Doyle's seven full-length historical novels, was to be an exercise in writing by a man who took both fiction and history seriously. Doyle's desire to write historical romances can be traced to the influence of Sir Walter Scott, for not only had Scott been Doyle's favorite childhood author, he was also the writer who, earlier in the century, had rejuvenated the form of the historical novel.[1] The critical and popular reception of Scott's novels established the historical novel as worthy of serious literary attention, and although Scott and Charles Kingsley (the author of many historical novels including *Westward Ho!* [1885]) were now dead and Charles Reade (the best-selling author of *The Cloister and the Hearth* [1861]) was an old man, Rider Haggard, R.D. Blackmore, and Robert Louis Stevenson had all written novels whose popularity attested to the continuing appeal of the conjunction of history and fiction.

Doyle, who aspired to be a serious writer, wanted to achieve this goal by following in Scott's footsteps, not only because he loved and respected that writer but also because since childhood he himself had felt and understood the appeal of this particular narrative form. The stories that his mother had told him, combining a love of the past, particularly the Middle Ages, with the form of the adventure story, was the kind of narrative most familiar and most beloved by him. It seems only natural that as he was waiting for *A Study in Scarlet* to be published, his thoughts should turn to the works of Sir Walter Scott and to his own desire to emulate that author.

Not all historical novels are romances. In several of Scott's novels, notably *Old Mortality, The Antiquary,* and *The Heart of Mid-Lothian,* the world of romance is largely subsumed in the author's realistic attempt to capture the lives of the lowland peasants in eighteenth-century Scotland. Significantly, though, Doyle loved best precisely those Scott novels, like *Ivanhoe,* that are romances. As Northrop

Frye has pointed out, "The romance is nearest of all literary forms to the wish fulfillment dream. . . . the child-like quality of romance is marked by its extraordinarily persistent nostalgia, its search for some kind of imaginative golden age in time or space."[2] Doyle desperately wanted to explore his own "imaginative golden age" in fiction, thus his historical novels are better defined as historical romances.

The appeal of the historical romance is—like the detective story and the adventure story—based on the reader's desire to escape the complexities of everyday life. These forms, or genres, provide such an escape because they are set apart from reality in worlds that are morally secure and closed. First as a listener and now as a narrator of tales, Doyle was attracted to these forms for those reasons, but he made a sharp distinction between them in terms of their literary value; detective and adventure stories provided pleasant, honest work, he thought, but historical novels were serious literary endeavors.

Thus, the ambitious author who had been accumulating books and information on the seventeenth century for two years, decided in 1887 to begin his most serious work: "I now determined to test my powers to the full and I chose a historical novel for this end, because it seemed to me the one way of combining a certain amount of literary dignity with those scenes of action and adventure which were natural to my young and ardent mind" (*MA*, 70).

As a child, his "ardent mind" had been further stimulated by the work of his favorite historian, Thomas Babington Macaulay, whose *History of England*[3] can be credited with providing Doyle with the subject of *Micah Clarke*. "I wish Macaulay had written a historical novel," Doyle was to write later, but, in fact, Doyle wrote the novel himself, using Macaulay's events as inspiration.[4] It was to the historian's stirring descriptions of the sombre soldier-preachers who followed Oliver Cromwell that Doyle owed his start: "I had always felt great sympathy for the Puritans who, whatever their little peculiarities, did represent political liberty and earnestness in religion" (*MA*, 18). These Puritan soldiers were to be the subject of his first historical work.

Micah Clarke

Micah Clarke is set in Scotland in 1685, when, under a Catholic king, James II, the Puritans were awaiting the call to arms of the

Protestant claimant to the throne, James, duke of Monmouth. The story, related forty-nine years later, is told by Micah to his three grandchildren. As the lengthy subtitle explains, this book is Micah's testament "wherein is contained a full report of certain passages in his early life, together with some account of his journey from Havant to Taunton with Decimus Saxon in the summer of 1685 also of the adventures that befell them during the Western rebellion, and of the intercourse with James, Duke of Monmouth, Lord Grey and other persons of quality."[5]

This introduction serves to anchor the story firmly in geographical place and time, while Micah's initial remarks, echoing Doyle's own sentiments, reassure the reader that the storyteller is more competent than any historian to deal with the narrative demands of such a structure: "I shall try to make those dead men quicken into life for your behoof, and to call back out of the mists of the past those scenes which were brisk enough in the acting, though they read so dully and so heavily in the pages of the worthy men who have set themselves to record them" (MC, 9).

Adventure is the one essential plot element in romance, and an element that is fully sustained in *Micah Clarke,* for once Micah leaves home, he is caught up by a continuous series of heroic adventures that move the narrative sequentially forward.[6] As in most heroic adventure stories, these episodes take place within the larger context of the marvelous journey—a journey that is both physical, as Micah travels the width of southern England, and spiritual and psychological, as Micah passes from boyhood to manhood.

The combination of militancy and fanaticism so characteristic of Cromwell's supports is exemplified by Micah's father, "Ironside" Clarke, a man given to visionary fits, who is described by Micah as being filled with "fierce and earnest religion" (MC, 13). As an example of the younger generation, Micah and his religious beliefs are more moderate, due, we are told, to the influence of his mother's Episcopalian belief. Even in the face of her husband's fervency she had "held to her religion with a quiet grip which was proof against every attempt to turn her from it" (MC, 16). The young Micah is thus presented as the product of both his father's moral rigidity and his mother's tolerance, while his faith, a result of this diversity and best described as benevolent humanism, transcends all sectarian divisions.

The "call to adventure,"[7] the summons to the hero that moves him to begin the quest, is, in this book, contained in a letter brought by a soldier of fortune, Decimus Saxon, to Micah's father. At first sight the substantial differences that lie between Micah and his father seem to set the stage for a generational conflict, but the potential conflict between father and son is moved to the larger world outside the home when Ironside Joe finds that he is too old to go to war. The summons meant for Joe is passed to the gentler Micah who rides off on his large gray horse, aptly named Covenant, to face the forces of religious fanaticism and of worldly vice on the battlefield of England.

Once he leaves home, Micah's heroism is immediately tested by Monmouth's messenger, Decimus Saxon, who had posed as a Puritan zealot while in Ironside Joe's home but who, as soon as they are on the road, drops his Puritan language and behavior. Decimus shows himself to be a true soldier of fortune, one willing to fight for any side providing he stands to gain by it: "It is nothing to me whether James Stuart or James Walters sits upon the throne but the court and army of the King are already made up. Now since Monmouth hath both courtiers and soldiers to find it may well happen that he may be glad of my services and reward them with honourable preferment." Saxon's mercenary motives are placed in sharp contrast to Micah's integrity: "My folk," he responds quickly, "have always fought for the liberty of the people and the humbling of tyranny" (*MC,* 96–97).

The conflict between the two men flares into open hostility on the first night, when Decimus wants to steal gold from an alchemist who has befriended them. At first Micah contents himself with physically defending the treasure, warning: "if you should attempt it I shall lay you on your back," but the next day he follows this up with the moral censure of abandoning Decimus, because, as he explains, "You are no fit company for honest men" (*MC,* 102). This punishment, indicative of Micah's attitude throughout, is a salutary one for Decimus. He learns from Micah's ideals and ends up calling the younger man "Master Morality" while promising to "unlearn some of the tricks of my trade" (*MC,* 105).

Following the format of the romance, the hero continues to be given various tests. In the second one Micah proves his physical strength by engaging in a hand-wrestling contest with a powerful German soldier, who has a grip "which no man in the Palatinate would exchange" (*MC,* 199). After deliberately losing the first round in order to learn his adversary's tricks, Micah demands a rematch, which he wins. The English company is overjoyed; they give him the public acclaim indicative of his new stature. " 'We breed brawn in England as well as in Bradenburg,' said Saxon, who was shaking with laughter over the German soldier's discomfiture. 'Why, I have seen that lad pick up a full-size sergeant of dragoons and throw him into a cart as though he had been a clod of earth' " (MC, 200).

Having demonstrated moral courage and physical ability, Micah's third test is one that calls for a blend of caution and boldness. In a move calculated to undercut the strength of the opposing forces, Monmouth determines to send a message to the powerful duke of Beaufort asking him to change sides and fight for the claimant. Micah immediately volunteers for the task: "My father bade me spare neither life nor limb in this quarrel, and if this honourable council think that the duke may be gained over, I am ready to guarantee that the message shall be conveyed to him if men and horse can do it" (MC, 311). After a series of adventures that include a run-in with smugglers, a sea fight, and an escape from the infamous Boteler Dungeon, Micah delivers the message safely and returns a hero to Monmouth's army.

Micah's final test brings him full circle, for once again at the end of the book, he pits his decency and tolerance against Saxon's anarchic nature. This occurs at the end of the battle after a savage fight when Micah and Decimus have wounded their pursuers. Decimus, white with anger, wants to kill them. Once again, Micah defends what he knows to be right, namely, that one must not kill defenseless men, against his friend's animal-like behavior. As Micah recounts it, their argument went like this: " 'Nay, nay! Blood enough hath been shed' said I, 'let them lie.' 'What mercy would they have had upon us?' he cried, passionately, struggling to get his wrist free. 'They have lost, and must pay forfeit.' 'Not in cold blood,' I said firmly. 'I shall not abide it' " (MC, 345).

Thus, by distinguishing between when it is honorable to kill his enemies and when it is dishonorable, Micah resolves the conflict between the need for physical action at a dangerous time and the need for Christian charity. Micah is an active hero, one who does not hesitate to fight or kill if the occasion warrants. He does not like violence and he counsels against it whenever possible, but if he has to fight, on his own or anyone else's behalf, he does so courageously and skillfully. Doyle, in fact, revels in the need for action, as his descriptions of the scenes of battle show. To fail to take action or to miss the right moment for doing so would bring dishonor on the participant; therefore it is essential that the hero of these novels be physically able and aggressive whenever the situation demands. Micah is such an active hero, yet he is one whose conscience is as active as his body. The episodes of physical testing are important precisely because those episodes also make a definite moral point. The violence that Micah and his friends indulge in is justified as the proper response to a chaotic historical period only as long as their reasons for doing so are "worthy." Violence that is indulged in for base reasons, ones motivated by feelings of revenge or of cruelty, must not be allowed, for those are the very acts that bring the hero dishonor.

The heroic virtues that Micah embodies are the best that England can produce. Further, because he is young and pure of heart, Micah does not embody the leftover heroism of a bygone age; this kind of heroism is left to Micah's courtly friend from London, Sir Gervas Jerome. So persuasive is Jerome's heroism that some critics have suggested that he is the true hero of this novel.[8] Gervas's death scene is, in fact, the traditional one of the gallant soldier. In response to Micah's offer of escape, Micah tells us: "He looked up smiling and shook his head. 'I stay with my company,' said he. 'Your company,' Saxon cried. 'Why, man, you are mad! Your company is cut off to the last man.' 'That's what I mean,' he answered, flicking some dirt from his cravat. 'Don't ye mind! Look out for yourselves. Goodbye, Clarke' " (*MC*, 342).

The fact that Gervas's death is contrasted with Micah's escape from death, and further, that it is Micah who tries to save his friend, suggests, however, that Jerome is not the true hero here. Gallant and courageous as the knight is, he still epitomizes the old values. Ultimately, he is a member of a doomed aristocracy who can best serve England's interests by making way for the new order, the more democratic values exemplified by the artisans and workers who are Micah's friends. Sir Gervas is a nostalgic and doomed figure; Micah is not.

Micah Clarke, completed in only three months, was dedicated to Doyle's mother, the Ma'am, and sent out with high hopes on the part of the author: "If it comes off," he confessed in a letter to his favorite sister Lottie, "we may then, I think, take it as proved that I can live by my pen."[9] Doyle was still thinking of himself as a doctor, so that his writing, the "milk cow" as he termed it, was only a means to an end. Yet, at first it appeared as though even this means was to be denied him, for publisher after publisher, including his mentor and former editor James Payn, rejected the manuscript.

In a fortuitous move, however, Doyle sent the book in November 1888 to Robert Louis Stevenson's friend and editor, Andrew Lang, the Scottish poet and critic who had already published some of Doyle's short stories. Lang, one of the foremost admirers and defenders of the form of the romance, had published a manifesto on its behalf the previous year. The right author, Lang claimed in this essay, writing "an impossible romance," could "still win us from the newspapers and the stories of shabby love, and cheap remorses and commonplace failures."[10]

Happily for Doyle, Lang thought that *Micah Clarke* was such a work. The novel was immediately accepted by Lang and published by Longmans in February 1889. As it turned out, Andrew Lang's belief in Doyle's ability to woo the general reader back to heroic romances was completely justified. Not only did almost all the critics rave about *Micah Clarke,* but the book sold extremely well. Doyle, who earlier had talked about trying a long adventure story modeled on the work of Rider Haggard, was so buoyed by the success of *Micah Clarke* that he immediately started work on what was to be his own favorite story, *The White Company.*

The White Company

The White Company (1891), a story set in 1366, a time which saw the full flowering of knights and chivalry, was one of the few novels that Doyle became completely immersed in. He had developed the idea for this book in between medical rounds, familial responsibilities, short stories, and *Micah Clarke,* but when he decided to write *The White Company,* he put everything else aside and devoted himself to it in an unprecedented manner. The preceding Easter, he had gone to the New Forest for a brief holiday with three male friends. After walking in the New Forest, Doyle decided that he wanted to begin his story there, so, later that spring, he returned alone with a huge supply of books on the history, the heraldry, the social customs, clothing, manners, and speech of the fourteenth century. It was not until autumn of the same year that he returned to Southsea to his wife and to his nine-month-old daughter, Mary Louise, and he spent the next eleven months, an inordinate amount of time for this author, writing *The White Company*.

As in *Micah Clarke,* the story's protagonist, Alleyne Edricson, is a young man who embodies the qualities of innocence and chastity characteristic of the archetypal hero. But, unlike Micah who begins and ends the book by asserting his own version of Christianity, a humanistic version that will serve England and Englishmen better than either the fanaticism of the Puritans or the duplicity of the established Protestant Church of England, Alleyne, raised in the monastery of Beaulieu, is, as a product of the teachings of the monks, a religious young man. Alleyne's education, therefore, is to be in the ways of the world, ways which are opposed to the ways of the cloister. The characters who undertake Alleyne's worldly education are a small band of friends, a group of representative Englishmen, who, meeting him after he leaves the monastery, persuade him to go to fight the French under the banner of a venerable knight, Sir Nigel Loring.

The two friends who teach him most about the ways of the world and of society are John of Hordle and Samkin Aylward. Big John of Hordle, modeled after the Little John who appears in the tales of Robin Hood, had also been a novice at Beaulieu Abbey until he was dismissed from the order because he had broken three rules. First, he had drunk in one gulp the portion of beer allotted to four monks; second, after being reproved for blasphemy he had put the reprover face down in the fish pond; and third, in order to help a woman over a fast-flowing stream, "he did lift up the said Mary Sowley and did take, carry and convey her across."[11] The large, red-headed John loves life too much to be shut up in a monastery, and it is from him that Alleyne learns about the joy and zest of life.

The contrast at the ecclesiastical trial between the freedom-loving, self-assured John and his accusers, the timid, hypocritical monks, illustrates one of Doyle's central themes, that the monks, instead of serving God, are serving the selfish, materialistic aims of the ambitious dignitaries of the church. From the first moment, the reader is told that John is aligned with all things natural: "His cowl thrown back upon his shoulders, and his gown robes unfastened at the top, disclosed a round, sinewy neck, ruddy and corded like the bark of the fir. Thick, muscular arms, covered with a reddish down, protruded from the wide sleeves of his habit, while his white skirt, looped up upon one side, gave a glimpse of a huge knotty leg, scarred and torn with the scratches of brambles." The monk, "a lean, white-faced brother who appeared to be ill at ease, shifting his feet from side to side and tapping his chin nervously" (*WC*, 4), stands in sharp opposition to the confident defendant. The difference between the muscular Christian embracing the world with all its difficulties and the ratlike servant of God who turns his back on the world illustrates Doyle's principal concern in *The White Company*.

Doyle's position in *The White Company* is that organized religion, the hierarchy of the church, is oppressing the very people that it should serve. The men who believe in Christianity (that is, a direct application of the lessons of Christ's life, not the form of Christianity practised by the medieval church) are naturally close to God, for their religion lives in their hearts and minds. As examples of this, John of Hordle, Alleyne Edricson, and Samkin Aylward all carry God with them; they are Christians at heart so they do not need to have Christianity interpreted for them. Pierre Nordon has pointed out that Doyle believes in "the spiritual benefit of action,"[12] and in *The White Company* the way that the friends act in the world, both in peace and in war, is held up as the spiritual standard, a standard that is clearly in contrast to the pious morality of the passive monks at Beaulieu.

The second friend and tutor to Alleyne is Samkin Aylward, one of those English archers who made the longbow an intrinsic part of fourteenth-century warfare. Samkin is forty years old, a seasoned veteran of the French wars, a master bowman, and a womanizer. Described as being of medium build, he has "extraordinary breadth of shoulder, well marked features in a deeply tanned face" and eyes that "were bright and searching, with something of menace and authority in their quick glitter . . . as befitted one who was wont to set his face against danger" (*WC*, 35).

Aylward, the hardened campaigner, spends the time in between battles bringing his captured loot back to England and chasing every woman who crosses his path: " 'Hola! a woman by my soul!' he says, "and in an instant he had clipped Dame Eliza round the waist and was kissing her violently. His eye happening to wander upon the maid, however, he instantly abandoned the mistress and danced off after the other" (*WC*, 43). The naive Alleyne is at first confused by the mixture of vice and virtue in Samkin's character: "Men had been good or had been bad in his catalogue, but here was a man who was fierce one minute and gentle the next, with a curse on his lips and a smile in his eye. What was to be made of such a man as that?" (*WC*, 45).

What Alleyne does finally make of Samkin Aylward is that—like the rest of mankind—the archer is both good and bad, that is, he is human. The important lesson for Alleyne is that both John of Hordle and Samkin Aylward love life and manage to enjoy it while still striving to be responsible men. John finds his place in the world by becoming a good soldier and Samkin finally stops his philandering to marry the mistress Eliza and settle down as the prosperous innkeeper of "The Pied Merlin."

Parallel to the three friends yet superior to them in terms of age and rank are the three knights that they serve: the thin, Don Quixote–like figure of Sir Nigel Loring, the robust gourmet Sir Oliver Butteshorn, and the one-eyed, seasoned veteran, Sir John Chandos. These three knights fulfill the functions of the archetypal wise men who frequent the pages of romances, but, whereas in earlier stories these characters might have been imbued with magical powers, in *The White Company* they act simply as the teachers of the standards of the chivalric age. Because their form of knightly behavior belongs to an age that is over, their lessons are not always valuable ones, however. Sir Nigel Loring, who is forever looking for "fortune to send him a venture" (*WC*, 140), a knightly exchange or deed by which he would win some personal honor, is told—in no uncertain terms—by Prince Edward that sometimes notions of personal honor must give way to the needs of the larger body politic. True to the absolute demands of the chivalric code, Sir Nigel urges the prince to stick to a vow made in a foolish moment even though it was a mistake, and even though it would cost the prince dearly. Nigel is too old to learn the lesson implicit in the princely rebuke—although in this instance he has to succumb—but Alleyne and his comrades are not. They have to learn that sometimes it is necessary to sacrifice their desire for personal honor in the service of the greater social good. Sir Nigel exemplifies the rigidity of the old heroic code, while the next generation has to learn to practice intelligent restraint as a means to achieving the collective good.

The plot of *The White Company*, a plot which includes Alleyne's fight with his evil older brother, a battle at sea with Norman pirates, a knight's tournament at which an unknown Black Knight defeats all five of England's bravest warriors, a defense of a castle under

siege, and a fierce fight with the Spanish in which the White
Company itself gains eternal honor, is exciting enough to capture
any reader's imagination. But the most compelling part of the novel
has to do with the struggle of Alleyne and his band of comrades to
maintain their standards of honor and decency in a world that does
not always understand or care about the difference between good
and evil. This struggle, of course, has mythic dimensions. Alleyne's
triumph over passivity, hypocrisy, and brutality reminds us, as
Doyle intends it to, of the struggles of Ulysses, of St. George, of
Lancelot, and of all mythic heroes.

Alleyne's relationship with the women in *The White Company,*
and in particular with the daughter of the knight he serves, the
lovely Lady Maude Loring, is the one expected by readers of romance.
Lady Maude, whose love Alleyne has to win, is the person whose
vulnerability, whose need for love and protection, provides the impetus for his action. And Alleyne carries with him her scarf as a
visible symbol of what he has to attain. Unlike the heroes of many
romances, however, Alleyne does not have to learn self-restraint;
his path of duty is not one of self-control but one of self-expansion
so that, while still remaining a Christian, he can experience life in
all its complexity. His ability to win the lady of pleasure, to participate in love and marriage, is, therefore, measured by the distance
that he travels from the world of the death-dealing monks.

Alleyne's return, just seconds before Maude, who believes him
dead, enters a nunnery, provides a dramatic context for the reconciliation of the lovers and a satisfying resolution to the dichotomy
between the monastery and the world, monk and knight, death and
life that the novel has established. As a knight Alleyne has chosen
to live in the world, as a lover he has to prevent his lady's incar-
ceration in the very institution that he has already rejected.

Doyle portrays Maude's entrance into the nunnery as a form of
death, for her figure "garbed in white" and "wreathed in white
blossoms" suggests a corpse, while the church building, wherein
"dank, cold air comes out from the black arch" (*WC,* 360), is clearly
the tomb itself. Alleyne, who has reached the end of his journey
and now stands for love and sexual life, is contrasted to the female
attendants "who have ever been taught that the way of nature is
the way of sin," and who are ushering Maude into the vault. This
passage, with its overtones of Orpheus and Eurydice, ends happily
as the young knight literally scatters the procession of virginal

novices before barring the door to the tomb-church with his own body.

Once the reconciliation is complete and the lovers are physically united, "his arms around her drooping body and her wet cheek upon his breast" (*WC*, 360), nature welcomes them back from the sexual death of the convent: "The sun shines bright and the birds are singing amid the ivy on the drooping branches" (*WC*, 361); while their marriage celebrates the completion of Alleyne's journey from monkish celibacy to life and to love. Indeed, the ceremony that marks their marriage also marks Alleyne's final rite of passage from boyhood to manhood and therefore marks the final defeat for the death-dealing practices of the church. Alleyne's triumph is the triumph of life itself.

In the final pages, Doyle reiterates and emphasizes his position on organized religion. The church, he asserts, is a greedy, tyrannical institution that has forgotten, in its lust for power, the true meaning of Christ's teachings. Yet he also maintains that the future of Christianity is not all black, for the ending of *The White Company* suggests that if we cannot put our faith in the official emissaries of God's word, we can and must put our faith in the kind of muscular Christianity that lies at the heart of the knightly code of behavior. *The White Company* expresses Doyle's belief that honorable behavior, the impulse to protect all those who are weak and helpless and to fight aggressively to see that justice is done, is "an article of faith which might strengthen and sustain as powerfully as any religion."[13] Doyle loved *The White Company* best precisely because in it he was able to enunciate his own creed, encapsulated in phrases like "Help to the helpless, whosoever shall ask for it," "Fearless to the strong; humble to the weak," "To give your word is to give a knightly pledge,"[14] through the actions of that small band of comrades whose antecedents are the great heroic figures of the mythic and historical past. In a moment of authorial exaltation over this story, he wrote to his sister: "You will be pleased, I am sure, to know that I have finished my great labour, and that *The White Company* has come to an end. The first half is very good, the second quarter pretty good, and the last quarter very good again. So rejoice with me, my dear, for I am as fond of Hordle John and Samkin Aylward and Sir Nigel Loring as though I knew them in the flesh, and I feel that the whole English-speaking race will come in time to be fond of them also."[15]

With some trepidation Doyle first sent the manuscript to his old friend and editor James Payn, the man who had earlier refused to publish *Micah Clarke*. To the author's great surprise and "everlasting joy,"[16] Payn not only wanted to publish the novel, he praised it extravagantly, suggesting that it was the best historical novel since *Ivanhoe*. To one who wanted to follow in Scott's footsteps, this was the greatest praise, and Doyle treasured it appropriately.

The reader and critic will have some trouble echoing Payn's position, however, for while *The White Company* is a good historical novel that contains wonderful passages, it is marred by various authorial inconsistencies which make any comparison to *Ivanhoe* seem excessive. Scott, as one critic has pointed out, "was a Jacobite at heart, though his patriotism and his common sense made him a faithful subject of the reigning king."[17] To turn Scott's position around, Doyle was at heart, first and foremost, a royalist, while his sense of fair play and decency made of him, in theory, a democrat. The more proficient novelist managed to find subjects that could accommodate both his heart and head, but the less expert Doyle often finds himself floundering in situations where his loyalties are opposed.

The White Company uses a wide social strata; tradespeople, yeomen, nobles, and peasants are all shown involved in the complex series of relationships that binds them together. The successful portrayal of the clash of those classes, the depiction of those moments in history when the ideology of the aristocracy is inimical to the ideology of the peasants, for example, demands a writer who is sure of where his sympathy lies.

One example from *The White Company* will suffice to illustrate this pervasive narrative difficulty. While the friends are riding over the marshes of France, the narrator comments, sympathetically, on the plight of the starving peasants, those "strange lean figures scraping and scratching amid the weeds and thistles" whose land has been "ten times harried" to raise the ransom money for their feudal lord. The narrator, seeming to understand the plight of the peasants, explains: "Yet why should they build and strive, when the first adventurer who passed would set torch to their thatch, and when their own feudal lord would wring from them with blows and curses the last fruits of their toil" (*WC*, 261). Further, the narrator ends with a timely warning to the oppressive nobility, "when such men who are beyond hope and fear, begin in their dim minds to see the source of their woes, it may be an evil time for those who have wronged them."

Yet, that very night when the "Brushwood folk" attack the castle, the narrator's sympathies abruptly change. The peasants, described as "fierce," "wild," "murderers" complete with "flashing teeth," "bristling hair," and "mad leapings and screamings," become sub-human. These wretches, with no feelings or indeed any discernible human trait, are so bestial that the heroic knights are able to kill them mercilessly. "In front of the central guest-chamber stood DuGuesclin and Sir Nigel, half-clad and unarmoured, with the mad joy of battle gleaming in their eyes. Their heads were thrown back, their lips compressed, their blood-stained swords poised over their right shoulders and their left feet thrown out. Three dead men lay huddled together in front of them: while a fourth, with the blood squirting from a severed vessel, lay back with updrawn knees, breathing in wheezy gasps" (*WC*, 262).

While Scott's sympathy would have been consistently with the peasantry, the poor, and the dispossessed, even when they acted brutally or when the historical moment was clearly against them, Doyle, trapped within his ideal of what is an aristocratic knightly code, is only certain that no group of peasants could sustain that code. Therefore, although he despises the changes in feudalism instigated (in this case) by the breakdown of noblesse oblige, he is far from advocating rebellion for the peasants. What he wants is a return to the old social ties where kindliness and responsibility characterize the relationship between lord and peasant. The discrepancy in the text between the narrator's initial view of the down-trodden peasants and Sir Nigel's high-handed dismissal of them as "curs" and "dogs" reflects a discrepancy in Doyle's view of the world that is not easy to reconcile.

Nevertheless, *The White Company* was an immediate popular success. Initially put out in the usual three-decker style, the first edition was quickly sold out, as were the more than fifty editions of the novel then published in a single volume. Though Doyle was extremely pleased that the public liked what he felt was his most memorable achievement, when he finished writing he was introspective and depressed. He felt as though *The White Company* had said everything that he wanted to say; he had done what he set out to do and he was finished.

Characteristically unable to live with any form of indecision or ambiguity, Doyle turned back to medicine in an effort to redirect his energies. To this end, he determined to go to Vienna (where, contrary to popular belief, he did not meet Freud) to train to be an eye specialist. But ironically this decision served only to lead him back to his career as a writer, for by the following year—August 1891—he had had not one eye patient, he had been critically ill with pneumonia, and, in the aftermath of both these events, had decided to live by his writings. Within a few months of his return, he had again turned his attention to a third historical novel: *The Refugees*.

The Refugees

The Refugees, begun in December 1891 at the same time that Doyle was writing the second series of six Holmes stories, was finished early in 1892. Doyle was a well-established writer by this time, so the novel was immediately accepted for publication as a serial in *Harper's* magazine. It ran from January to December 1893 and was published as a book by Longmans in July 1893.

Set in 1685, *The Refugees* has a plot that moves from the French court of Louis the Fourteenth to the forests of Canada as a band of French Huguenot refugees flees from their homeland only to find themselves in the middle of the French-Indian war. Originally, Doyle had wanted to reintroduce Micah Clarke and Decimus Saxon as characters in his new novel, but he soon decided that was too difficult and concentrated instead on two new characters: Armory DeCatinat, a Protestant Frenchman serving as a captain of the King's Guard and an American, Amos Green, a woodsman and explorer of the New World. The scenes of the Iroquois attacks in the forest are modeled on James Fenimore Cooper's Leatherstocking tales, while the history is based on the work of the American historian James Parkman.

The Franco-Canadian novel is not one of Doyle's best historical novels, possibly because during this period he was under constant pressure to produce more and more Holmes stories. His enthusiasm for this book was, in any event, never very strong, and he seems with *The Refugees* to have come as close to writing a "page-turner" as it was possible for him to do. In a letter to his sister, discussing his treatment of the intrigues at the court of Louis the Fourteenth he admits this: "My word, my word, I give the reader his six shillings worth of passion! . . . Talk about love-scenes! It is volcanic."[18] In spite of these passages the author's own verdict of himself as "fairly satisfied" is perhaps the best overall judgment of *The Refugees*.

The Lesser Three: *The Great Shadow*, *Rodney Stone*, and *Uncle Bernac*

During the next four years, Doyle wrote three more historical novels and a number of short stories featuring the infamous Brigadier Gerard. These stories, first published in book form as *The Exploits of Brigadier Gerard* (1896) with a second later series appearing as *The Adventures of Gerard* (1903), won a wide audience. The historical period is still Napoleonic France, but rather than historical romances, these stories are comic adventure stories, featuring Etienne Gerard, a colonel of the Hussars of Conflans, a man capable of heroism, yet one whose chief characteristic is that of being "gloriously ridiculous."[19] Gerard's self-satisfaction, his boasting, his narcissistic blindness, all combine to satirize the heroic qualities that he epitomizes and to place Gerard firmly in the grand tradition of heroic buffoons.

Doyle's next full-length historical romance, *The Great Shadow*, was commissioned by Arrowsmith, in the spring of 1892, to appear as a novel in their Christmas annual. The book was probably finished by midsummer of that year. The "shadow" of the title refers to Napoleon Bonaparte, and the book ends with the Battle of Waterloo, a battle where the "shadow" that lay over all Europe was finally dissipated by the English forces. As five of his ancestors had fought there and his mother had awarded the battle a central part in her stories of family history, Doyle had a deep personal interest in Waterloo. And perhaps partly as a result of his early and long familiarity with this event, he made the battle scene, complete with the gun smoke that effectively blinds, deafens, and stifles the men of the 71st Highlanders the best in the book. The sheer confusion of such a battle, the panic of the men and horses, the sense of unreality that permeates the atmosphere, and the immediacy of the life-and-death struggle when the French do suddenly appear out of the smoke, are all captured in this one chapter with the greatest skill.

The next novel, *Rodney Stone,* serialized in the *Strand* and published as a novel by Smith Elder and Co., was finished at the end of 1895. This book, set in the time of the Regency, is a tribute to the art of prizefighting. The England of dandies, gaming parlors, high-waymen, the England of gentlemen who would match their horses and their carriages against each other in a race on the public road from Brighton to London, are all vividly evoked as background to the rise of Boy Jim, a simple blacksmith's son who becomes one of the best prizefighters of his day. This novel is very uneven, but so great was Doyle's reputation by this time that he was given an advance of four thousand pounds for the novel and an equally surprising advance of fifteen hundred pounds for the serial rights.

Uncle Bernac, begun in 1896, was Doyle's least favorite work. He knew from the time that he began writing or "labouring" as he characterized his activity, that this book was to be a failure. Planned as a short novel, *Uncle Bernac* yet "cost me more than any big book. I never seem to be quite in the key, but I must slog through it somehow."[20]

Unfortunately, *Uncle Bernac* shows all the defects of such authorial slogging. Set in Napoleonic France at the point when Napoleon's Grand Army was at Boulogne preparing for the invasion of England, the story simply never develops. Doyle's greatest difficulty is that he is not sure whether Napoleon, his chief protagonist, is "a great hero or a great scoundrel"[21] so the participation of the hero, Louis, in Boney's service is fundamentally problematic. Unlike the figure of Cromwell in *Micah Clarke,* the ambitious narcissistic Corsican soldier is not a character that Doyle respects or admires. As an indication of Doyle's xenophobic confusion, Napoleon is variously described as a dictator, a womanizer, a poet, a cruel manipulator, and a child, while further on he appears as terrible, charming, wolflike, intelligent, and measured.[22] So troublesome is this conflict that the book degenerates, after the first hundred pages, into what is a historical exercise in portraiture, a portrait which Doyle achieves by simply recreating several days in Napoleon's life.

To the careful reader, *Uncle Bernac* suggests that Doyle was tired of the form of the historical novel. Apparently, there *was* nothing further that he wanted to say. It seems as though Doyle was being personally astute about his lack of interest in the form when, at the end of *Uncle Bernac,* he apologizes to the reader for the verbose coverage of Louis' troubles: "You have already heard more of them perhaps than you care for" (*Bernac,* 307).

The Last and Best: *Sir Nigel*

However, in 1904, fourteen years after *The White Company* appeared, Doyle undertook his last and best historical novel, one that was to act as a chivalric companion to *The White Company*—*Sir Nigel*. As the title indicates, the hero of this work is Nigel Loring, but the novel is not a sequel to *The White Company;* instead it is set some forty years before *The White Company* at a time when the young Nigel Loring, the venerable knight/teacher to Alleyne Edricson in the earlier book, is himself approaching manhood.

Like *The White Company, Sir Nigel* begins with a scene in a monastery where a single culprit is about to be severely punished by the ecclesiastical might of the large and powerful Abbey of Waverley. On first reading, these opening scenes are almost identical, for the crimes of the transgressor are very small in comparison to the power and greed of the abbey, but in fact the opening scene at Waverley suggests the central difference between the two novels. In *The White Company,* the culprit is John of Hordle, a character whose expulsion from the abbey sets the stage for the coming together of the band of comrades. Hordle, with his love for life, is not compatible with the sickly monks, and their parting is relatively painless. But in *Sir Nigel* the young hero himself is the innocent victim of blatant religious greed and intolerance. Unlike *The White Company,* which examines the relationship of a group of friends to the society they serve, *Sir Nigel* concentrates on a single individual, the young Nigel who, as Nordon suggests, "gives us the impression of controlling his own fate to the fullest limits allowed by freedom of the will."[23] Nigel's confrontation with the ecclesiastical hierarchy is thus made more terrible since he stands alone in the struggle between good and evil.

Similarly, the picaresque elements of *The White Company* are subsumed in *Sir Nigel* to the demands of a plot that revolves around Nigel Loring's vow to do three great deeds before returning to England to claim the hand of the "grave featured" Mary Buttesthorn.[24] The serial adventures of the friends of the White Company are replaced in *Sir Nigel* by the quest of a single hero whose journey serves to emphasize both a love of individual freedom and what Nordon calls "the code of chivalry in action."[25]

Initially, Nigel personifies only the former. We hear of his putting pike in the abbot's carp pond as revenge against the tyrannical abbey and of his "mishandling the messenger" who comes to summon him to his trial (*Nigel*, 47). Nigel's boyish attempts to wreak vengeance on the church are about to be severely punished when, at the very moment when the Lorings stand to lose their remaining few acres, the secular might of the king is interposed between the abbot and Nigel. The arrival of the king's messenger at Waverley also presages a movement from local to national affairs, a movement which heralds the start of Nigel's adventure.

Before Nigel sets out on his marvelous quest for adulthood and honor, he must, as all heroes must, be equipped with the weapons that he will need. While his father's armor is clearly too big for the youthful Nigel, he wears it nonetheless and so impresses the great knight Sir John Chandos with his audacity and skill that he is given "a bag of gold pieces" which he uses to buy a cunningly woven suit of armor, "that very suit for which he had yearned" (*Nigel*, 113–114).

The winning of a war horse is a more complicated matter and one that pits Nigel's strength and spirit against the unruly "yellow horse of Crooksbury" (*Nigel*, 14). The horse is as much an outsider in the placid everyday life of the village as Nigel is himself, while his proportions suggest a destiny that will parallel the young knight's: "Fetlock deep in the lush grass there stood a magnificent horse, such as a sculptor or a soldier might thrill to see. His color was a light chestnut with mane and tail of a more tawny tint. Seventeen hands high, with a barrel and haunches which bespoke tremendous strength he fired down to the most delicate lines of dainty breed in neck and crest and shoulder" (*Nigel*, 17).

In a passage familiar to every reader of romance and adventure and one that presages the hero's own experience, Nigel appears just as the great horse is about to savage a monk who has dared to try to capture the wild horse: "his head craned high, his ears erect, his mane bristling, his red nostrils opening and shutting with wrath, and his flashing eyes turning from side to side in haughty menace and defiance" (*Nigel*, 17).

Traditionally, when such an animal appears in older tales it has magical properties, but here it is only the simple monks, representing the uninitiated, who believe that the horse has supernatural origins: "the Devil is loose in the five-virgate field!" (*Nigel*, 13). Nigel, however, recognizing the same qualities in the horse that he prizes in himself, understands immediately that the horse is superior not supernatural. In a six-page passage that is clearly symbolic, Nigel masters the wild animal by riding it until they both drop exhausted on the ground. "You are my horse, Pommers," Nigel whispered, and he laid his cheek against the craning head. "I know you, Pommers, and you know me, and with the help of Saint Paul we shall teach some other folk to know us both" (*Nigel,* 28).

The recognition scene in which Nigel first names the horse, then claims him for his own, then walks side by side with him as an equal back to the village, is the scene in which Nigel attains the status of hero because the conquest of the horse represents the beginning of his conquest of his own destructive passions. In the battle for mastery both horse and rider are cleansed of their hate and anger, but only the horse has—as yet—learned to bend his will to another's commands.

The lesson that Nigel quickly teaches Pommers, to accept the idea of freedom within restraint, is one that Nigel learns more slowly. The lesson is first clearly enunciated by Sir John Chandos even before Nigel begins his quest. Speaking of some of his own early encounters, Chandos terms them "follies" and when Nigel hotly disputes this, crying, "Are they not the means by which honorable advancement may be gained and one's lady exalted," Chandos lectures him on the need for control and moderation: "But as one grows older and commands men, one has other things to think of. One thinks less of one's own honour and more of the safety of the army" (*Nigel,* 63–64).

Nigel accomplishes the first task of the three that he vowed to perform for the honor of St. Catherine and the Lady Mary when he helps lead a secret attack on a castle held by the French. The squire's second task, however, leads him to make exactly the mistake that Chandos had warned him against. In the heat of the battle, Nigel gives in to his notion of personal honor and leads a group of English archers in a suicidal attempt to break down the door that guards the entrance to the moat. Nigel's reasons are personal, chivalric ones, "for our fair ladies' sake" (*Nigel,* 257), but as a result of his misplaced heroism seven archers are killed and thirteen men at arms wounded. Knolles is furious and threatens to send Nigel ignominiously back to England: "Who was he, a raw squire, that he should lead an attack without orders? See what his crazy knight errantry had brought about?" (*Nigel,* 260).

Nigel finally manages to exonerate himself but not until, accepting the blame, he has chastised himself: "he withdrew apart, threw himself down amongst the bushes, and wept the hottest tears of his life, sobbing bitterly with his head between his hands" (*Nigel*, 260). Nigel's own cleansing tears presage his "breaking-in" period wherein his idea of anarchic freedom dies and a form of freedom, one that can be disciplined to the needs of other people, is born. When Nigel does return to the castle to rescue a friend, he does so without any thought of personal gain. And he wins honor precisely because his act was not motivated by base desire.

In an incident that demonstrates that he has learnt the chivalric lesson of unselfishness Nigel's third task is accomplished when he captures John, king of France, but does not want to gain the honor of holding him for ransom. Nigel's duty as a squire demands that he be at his master's side at all times so, after capturing the king, he leaves John of France on the battlefield while he carries out his squire's duties. Nigel's humility and "greatness of soul"[26] are thus rewarded with a knighthood.

The wedding of Nigel and Mary provides the traditional celebratory end to the romance, with the final blessing being given by Mary's father: "Now, take an old man's blessing, and may God keep and guard you both, and give you your desert, for I believe in my soul that in all this broad land there dwells no nobler man nor any woman more fitted to be his mate!" (*Nigel*, 344).

Although the story of Nigel is completed with that, Doyle has not finished. In a final authorial exhortation, he emphatically binds the present to the past: "And yet even gnawing time has not eaten all things away. Walk with me toward Guilford, reader, upon the busy highway. Here, where the high green mound rises before us, mark yonder roofless shrine which still stands four-square to the winds. It is St. Catherine's where Nigel and Mary plighted their faith" (*Nigel*, 345). This suggestion, that the past is an enduring part of the present and that its influence is still strong (the shrine, "four-square to the winds"), shows that one of Doyle's motives in writing this book was to remind his readers of England's glorious past in an effort to encourage them to come to grips with their contemporary problems.

The end returns the reader full circle to the beginning of *Sir Nigel*, to a country struggling to reconstitute itself after the awful devastation caused by the Black Death. We are told that in the period following this dreadful plague, at such a time of crisis, a different, freer England was being formed. Although *Sir Nigel* begins with this, the full import of this framing device is not felt until the end, when Doyle states that such a time has come again and that the heroism of the past must serve as an example and inspiration for present-day Englishmen and women. Like Shakespeare's histories, which stress the need to recognize the precise nature of the historical moment and to act quickly and decisively when that time demands, Doyle's conclusion warns the British people that the time for such action is come again. He does not specify any actual problem or point to any particular crisis, but he is talking about a world where all the many problems of postindustrialism were beginning to surface. As the old safe standards associated with Victorianism faded away, Doyle expressed his anxiety about what the twentieth century would mean to England.

Sir Nigel is an expression of that anxiety contained in a hymn to the past, a hymn which also serves as a call to English men and women to be as strong in this time of change as their ancestors:

The body may lie in mouldering chancel, or in crumbling vault, but the rumor of noble lives, the record of valor and truth can never die, but lives on in the soul of the people. Our own work lies ready to our hands; and yet our strength may be the greater and our faith the firmer if we spare an hour from present toils to look back upon the women who were gentle and strong, or the men who loved honor more than life on this green stage of England where for a few short years we play our little part." (*Nigel*, 346)

Chapter Five

The Return of Holmes

The ten years, 1893 to 1903, that elapsed between Holmes's ostensible fall into the Reichenbach Falls and his resurrection were eventful and prosperous ones for his creator. The man who had desperately needed every penny produced by his writings to pay his grocery bills was now, in 1903, not only one of the world's best-known authors, but also one of the world's highest-paid writers. Given Doyle's financial and artistic success and the tremendous relief that he had previously felt when he killed Holmes off, it is not immediately clear why he did finally accept the American offer of five thousand dollars for each new Holmes story up to six—or as many as he cared to write.

Doyle's life was, at this time, very expensive. He had two growing children, a large new house in Surrey, innumerable travel expenses for the whole family, as well as the costs attendant on Touie's worsening illness. Yet given the success of the rest of his work, the financial explanation for Holmes's return simply does not make sense. The more likely possibility, and one that is borne out by the fact that he continued to write Holmes stories up until his death, is that his dislike of the character had abated. Further evidence for this is found in the fact that he had actually picked Holmes, apparently without consulting anyone or succumbing to any outside pressure, to act as the problem solver in *The Hound of the Baskervilles.* This novel, published in 1901, takes place before Holmes's supposed death, so it does not count as a resurrection of Holmes, but it *is* a story in which the author chose Holmes to integrate the narrative. By making this choice, Doyle seems to acknowledge the literary and personal value of a developed, familiar character who can be counted on to bring order out of chaos and provide a much-needed "temporary release from doubt and guilt."[1]

Doyle's mood at the period was, according to his letters, one "of calm cynicism."[2] His wife's illness made demands that were debilitating for both of them, while his love for Jean Leckie, so long and honorably maintained, must have put an almost unbearable emotional strain on him. Professionally, his fervor to write (specifically his desire to write historical novels) and his desire for literary fame had been achieved so that, left with no immediate goal, no burning ambition unfulfilled, Doyle felt weary. One of his strongest characteristics—his optimism—was now strained by the anxieties of middle age. Given this mood and the fact that he could no longer feel that Holmes would detract from his well-established literary reputation, it is not hard to understand why he would reach for a form and a character whose purpose is to comfort and reassure. That Doyle chose to use Holmes at this time and that the detective was associated with a period when Doyle was beginning his writing career and when the world appeared more hopeful is not a coincidence.

England and Englishmen and women had also changed during that ten-year span. The most obvious change, one which announced the end of an era and a way of life, was the death of Queen Victoria in January 1901. Doyle, who along with thousands of his fellow countrymen, had stood and watched the funeral procession go by, worried about the state of his country as it moved into the new century: "And England—how stands England?" he had asked, anguishing that "a dark road" lay ahead.[3]

In spite of Doyle's prophecy, some bright spots lay ahead, and one of them, for many members of the reading public, was the reappearance of Holmes, a character who had retained their loyalty undiminished by the passage of time. On the day that the first of the new short stories appeared, copies could not be printed fast enough to keep up with demand, while the lines of people waiting to buy one of the available copies went down streets and around corners. "The scenes at the railway-bookstands," wrote one lady who was present at the time, "were worse than anything I ever saw at a bargain-sale."[4] The *Westminster Gazette* spoke for everyone when they thankfully announced: "It is as we suspected. That fall over the cliff did not kill Holmes."[5] Holmes was triumphantly back from the dead, and the delight of his readers was so great that, although Doyle could and would make the detective retire to beekeeping on the Sussex downs, the character of Sherlock Holmes could not be killed off again.

The footprints of a gigantic hound

In March 1901 Doyle accompanied his friend Fletcher Robinson for a golfing holiday on Dartmoor. One wet afternoon when golf was out of the question, Robinson amused Doyle by telling him some of the local legends attached to the moor. One of these, which included the appearance of a spectral hound, so captured Doyle's fancy that before he left the hotel he had written to the Ma'am announcing his intention to do a "little book," called *The Hound of the Baskervilles,* which would be, he asserted, "a real creeper!"[6] He did not mention Sherlock Holmes in that letter, but as soon as he began to plot out the story, he knew that he would need somebody to solve the mystery: "So I thought to myself, why should I invent such a character when I had him already in the form of Holmes."[7] Four months later, the "little" story was finished and Doyle was proclaiming: "Holmes is at his very best, and it is a highly dramatic idea."[8]

Much of the success of *The Hound of the Baskervilles* is due to Doyle's solution to the narrative difficulty that had plagued him in the two earlier full-length detective novels: how to explain the complex and lengthy series of events that lead up to the crime without the use of long flashbacks or lengthy explanations that interrupt the story unbearably. *The Hound of the Baskervilles* avoids these pitfalls by appropriating the device that Wilkie Collins made use of in *The Moonstone;* the story is told from several different perspectives by several different narrative voices.

As usual, Watson begins by introducing the snug Baker Street rooms with the two men settled comfortably within. The arrival of a Mr. Mortimer signals the beginning of the adventure, an adventure, explained by Mortimer, a friend and neighbor of the deceased Sir Charles Baskerville, with the aid of a seventeenth-century manuscript which he reads in full. The bulk of the investigation is then narrated by Watson who is, nominally as it turns out, the detective in charge, with changes in his "voice" being occasioned by his written reports to Holmes—official, dry, and fact-filled—and by the entries that he writes in his diary which are more emotional and speculative. The denouement is proclaimed by Holmes, and the final scene, in which all the loose ends are tied up, returns the reader to the safety of Baker Street under the aegis of the original narrator, Watson. The plot of *The Hound of the Baskervilles* is thus kept moving briskly along.

Of all the Holmes stories, *The Hound of the Baskervilles* is the one that makes most use of the trappings of the Gothic horror story.

Just as the Gothic story uses the supernatural, vampires, werewolves, spirits, ghosts, et cetera, to generate fear in the reader, so in Doyle's novel the hound itself, the legendary killer of the Baskerville family, is for most of the book supposed to be supernatural. Dr. Mortimer, who is described by Holmes himself as "a trained man of science," cannot account for the creature in any other way: "I find that before the terrible event occurred several people had seen a creature upon the moor which corresponds with this Baskerville demon and which could not possibly be any animal known to science. They all agreed that is was a huge creature, luminous, ghastly and spectral" (*CH,* 2:681). While Holmes's rationalism stands in opposition to this interpretation, "The devil's agents may be of flesh and blood, may they not?" (*CH,* 2:684), even the arch-rationalist is shaken when he hears the hound on the moor: " 'Where is it?' Holmes whispered, and I knew from the thrill of his voice that he, the man of iron, was shaken to the soul" (*CH,* 2:743).

The possibility of a supernatural explanation for the existence of the hound is kept alive until the end when, in the foggy confrontation on the moor, Holmes and Watson come face to face with the hound for the first time. But even sight is not enough to dispel the ghostly image: "A hound it was . . . but not such a hound as mortal eyes have ever seen." Holmes's rationalism is not fully justified until first, they shoot it, and second, they find the phosphorescent paint that Stapleton had used to outline "its muzzle and hackles and dewlap—in flickering flame" (*CH,* 2:757).

As background to the ghostly hound, the dark, ivy-covered home of the Baskervilles (full of ancestral portraits, long shadowy passageways, and large desolate rooms), the deserted countryside, where the few scattered houses stand in contrast to the grim prison at Princetown, and the moor itself add additional fearful elements to this narrative. The moor, the treacherous Grimpen mire, is less an element than a fully formed Gothic character in its own right, complete with a face, malignant hand, voice, and hidden secrets. In an earlier short story, "The Adventure of the Copper Beeches," Holmes had denounced the countryside as a place where evil goes undetected, "the lowest and vilest alleys in London do not present a more dreadful record of sin than does the smiling and beautiful countryside," (*CH,* 1:323) and the great Grimpen mire which literally swallows people and ponies up without leaving any clue as to their whereabouts seems precisely to embody Holmes's warning. The mire clearly poses a new kind of threat to Holmes's ability to combat evil, for it represents a system not susceptible to rationalism.

As the arch-villain, Stapleton is in partnership with the moor; together they provide Holmes with one of his most stringent tests. The human being is the instigator of the plot against the Baskervilles, while the mire is the alien environment that Holmes presumably does not understand. In contrast, Stapleton does know how to read the treacherous environment, "But my tastes led me to explore every part of the country round, and I should think there are few men who know it better than I do." Because he is also a secretive and treacherous man, he recognizes the value of these qualities in his natural ally: "You never tire of the moor. You cannot think what wonderful secrets it contains. It is so vast, so barren and so mysterious" (CH, 2:707). Understanding the characteristics that are so familiar to him, Stapleton is thus able to penetrate to the heart of the death-dealing land.

The treacherous quicksands that cover the secrets of the mire horrify Watson, who turns "cold with horror" when he observes the death of a lost moor pony: "Then a long, agonized, writhing neck shot upward and a dreadful cry echoed over the moor" (CH, 2:708). Stapleton, his companion on this occasion, has "stronger nerves" and remains unmoved. His unconcern for the fate of an animal is, as in much of British fiction, a signal mark of villainy, a villainy ironically emphasized by Stapleton's statement that he is a "naturalist," who often proclaims his devotion to nature and all things natural. The "nature" that Stapleton serves is the same nature present in Holmes's "smiling countryside", a dangerous primal world unconquered by reason and unreached by civilization. Stapleton is a naturalist (his hobby is catching butterflies and putting them in a killing jar) because as a product of this world he is fully conversant with its death-dealing ways. In this sense, the great Grimpen moor is Holmes's "heart of darkness."

Both Stapleton and the mire are worthy adversaries to Holmes. The naturalist has "checkmated" Holmes even before they leave London, provoking the detective to assert that the friends have found a "foeman worthy of our steel." The evil mire is an extension of the terrible weather that bedevils Holmes when he is in the city. The countryside is a more potent environment for evil, so that in this novel when Holmes needs to see, he is blinded by an impenetrable fog: "so as the fog-bank flowed onward we fell back before it until we were half a mile from the house, and still that dense white sea, with the moon silvering its upper edge, swept slowly and inexorably on" (*CH,* 2:756).

As it happens, Holmes proves as capable of dealing with the forces of evil found in the countryside as he is in the city. The "tall thin man" seen by Watson one moonlit night "brooding like the spirit of the place" over the moor turns out to be Holmes. The power of reason, embodied in the great detective, has conquered nature. The detective has been so successful at detecting *one* of his enemies that he has been able to live, since the beginning of the investigation, undetected at the heart of the moor, a place that puts him in a prime position to engineer the defeat of his human adversary.

Stapleton's ending is a particularly apt one. As he flees across the mire from the justice that Holmes and Watson represent, he cannot see "which is the right path" and suffers the same fate as the moorland ponies that he had previously observed with such equanimity. Aligned with the moor in life, Stapleton is forever linked to the morass in death. "Somewhere in the heart of the great Grimpen Mire, down in the foul slime of the huge morass which had sucked him in, this cold and cruel-hearted man is forever buried" (*CH,* 2:760).

As in the earlier Holmes stories, Doyle uses the juxtaposition of light, suggesting the light of reason, and dark, standing for the forces of ignorance, to emphasize Holmes's ability to see and understand. The world of the moor is one of darkness and, ultimately, fog. The world of Baskerville Hall—the center of the mystery—is one of "shadow and gloom." Even the outside of the hall is associated with a coffinlike gloom; "draped in ivy, with a patch clipped bare here and there where a window or a coat of arms broke through the dark veil" (*CH,* 2:702). The threat that hangs over Sir Henry is implicit in the "long shadows" that "trailed down the walls and hung like a black canopy above him."

Metaphorically, a new piece of evidence is greeted as "a new light," but Watson—in his ignorance—claims that this clue only leaves "the darkness rather blacker than before." Watson is, of course, always in the dark waiting for Holmes, the bringer of reason, to enlighten him. Both Holmes and Watson are incapacitated by the fog, which prevents actual sight, although Holmes, who already sees part of the answer ("There are several points upon which we still want light—but it is coming all the same [*CH*, 2:741]), is able to use another sense—hearing—to offset his loss of eyesight. Deprived of sight, Holmes is not deprived of reason, so like the tracker from a James Fenimore Cooper novel, he drops to the ground and "listens" to his enemies approach. The "dark fears" and "shadowy surmises" that had "clouded our lives so long" are lifted by the light of Holmes's "clear and logical mind" so that in the morning with "the fog lifted" the pair can return to the comfort of the "blazing fire" that awaits them in their rooms at Baker Street.

At the time of the publication of *The Hound of the Baskervilles,* the question was: Had Holmes changed during his nine-year absence? While this storm of inquiry is now largely centered around the later stories, the evidence of *The Hound of the Baskervilles* does point to one important change, that is, Holmes's relationship with Watson, which is now warmer, more personal than heretofore. Indeed, the novel fully justifies Barzun's analysis of the appeal of this unequal friendship: "And by virtue of Doyle's almost unique success in giving a soul to the detective's partner—the common man—we have in the two a companion pair to Don Quixote and Sancho Panza, a contrast and concert capable of occupying our imagination apart from the tales in which the two figure."[9] In all other respects, though, Holmes and the nature of his mission remain unchanged. While Holmes's own origins are aristocratic, he continues to be the self-appointed guardian of middle-class values. As always, he works within the social order to conserve it. Sir Henry Baskerville is the prototypical country squire, a solid, industrious, respectable member of the upper middle class. He is "sturdily built" with "thick black eyebrows and a strong pugnacious face." With his "ruddy tinted tweed suit" and "the weather-beaten appearance of one who has spent most of his time in the open air," Henry Baskerville personifies the benevolence of the feudal concept of noblesse oblige, found in the landed gentry: "there was something in his steady eye and the quiet assurance of his bearing which indicated the gentleman" (*CH*, 2:685).

Adept as Holmes is at defending this class of society, the story gives an additional reason why the Baskervilles must remain at Baskerville Hall; Henry Baskerville, like his Uncle Charles before him, has made enough money abroad to be able to restore and modernize the ancient property as well as to fulfill the traditional practice of providing employment for the villagers. Dr. Mortimer makes this point clear to Holmes in the initial interview: "It cannot be denied that the prosperity of the whole poor, bleak countryside depends upon his presence. All the good work which has been done by Sir Charles will crash to the ground if there is no tenant of the Hall" (*CH*, 2:682).

Holmes is not only saving the last male member of an illustrious family, and thus the family itself, he is, in a very real sense, saving England. In answer to the question, What will happen to England? Holmes is able to assure us that the younger sons who have left to make good in the outside world will be able to return safely to their ancestral homes and set about the task of rejuvenating England. Henry Baskerville's money will complete the new lodge house, install electricity at the Hall, and restore prosperity to the neighborhood. New money is returned to the old country when the younger sons take up the burdens of noblesse oblige and assure the safety of England.

In spite of the public's disappointment that Holmes had not yet been recalled to life, *The Hound of the Baskervilles* was an immediate success. The combination of the Gothic and the detective story, the different perspectives used to tell the story, and the closeness of the companionship evident between Holmes and Watson all add up to one of the most satisfying of the Holmes stories. Possibly Doyle was as pleased with Holmes's reappearance as Holmes's fans were. Whether Doyle also felt that the success of *The Hound of the Baskervilles* justified the further use of Holmes as a character is unclear. But at any rate, Doyle does not seem to have put up much of an argument when an American publisher suggested that Holmes should be resurrected in the form with which he was most closely associated, the short story.

The Return of Holmes

This new series of thirteen stories comprising "The Adventure of the Empty House," "The Norwood Builder," "The Dancing Men," "The Solitary Cyclist," "The Priory School," "Black Peter," "Charles Augustus Milverton," "The Six Napoleons," "The Three Students," "The Golden Pince-Nez," "The Missing Three-Quarter," "The Abbey Grange," and "The Second Stain," appeared consecutively in the *Strand* magazine from October 1903 until December 1904.

"The Adventure of the Empty House," the first story which marks

Holmes's return from the Reichenbach Falls, begins with a solitary
Watson trying desperately to maintain the tradition of Holmes.
Since Holmes's death, Watson insists he has "never failed to read
with care the various problems which came before the public (*CH*,
2:483). This particular problem is a locked-room mystery in which
young Ronald Adair has been found shot dead in a room that was
locked on the inside and provided no possibility of undetected escape
from the one window. The answer that he was shot through the
open window with an air gun is not one that Watson can hit upon
but the Adair case is less interesting than the return of the one
person who can explain the case, and the death of young Adair is
instantly subsumed by the atmosphere of surprise and excitement
that surrounds the return of the detective. The tie-in between the
two events is that the man who has committed the murder, Colonal
Moran, an erstwhile henchman of Professor Moriarty's, is also
Holmes's archenemy who has vowed to kill him. During the ten
years of Holmes's absence, he has been playing a cat-and-mouse
game with the remaining members of the Moriarty gang. As a result
of the continuing need for secrecy, Holmes has not contacted his
old friend, nor does he announce his return, so that Watson and
the reader are almost equally surprised when an irascible bookseller,
who is ostensibly trying to sell Watson a book on *British Birds*, is
magically transformed into the detective: "I rose to my feet, stared
at him for some seconds in utter amazement, and then it appears
that I must have fainted for the first and last time in my life" (*CH*,
2:485).

The Adair case now has to be quickly solved, for the capture of
Colonel Moran will mean that Holmes is free to reappear and assume
the role of public protector that he was forced to relinquish when
he went into hiding. Holmes has a double duty on this case. First,
he must, as he always does, remove the criminals from society and,
second, he must then actively restore the dispensation of justice by
taking up the duties and responsibilities of his role. Holmes's ironic
use of the sentimental phrase, "journeys end in lovers' meetings,"
a phrase that he utters to Moran after the latter's capture, is the
phrase that captures the real sentiment and the meaning of "The
Adventure of the Empty House." For it is Holmes's journey that
has ended in lovers' meetings. The detective is reunited with the
forces of evil in the symbiotic relationship that he has with his long-
time adversary, he is reunited with his professional responsibilities,

his former life, his companion in arms (who, like the traditional Victorian wife, faints from an excess of emotion), and, last but not least, he is reunited with his loyal readers, who, like patient lovers, waited without giving up hope for ten long years.

Some modern critics have claimed to be disappointed in the powers of the "new" Holmes as they were demonstrated in the batch of thirteen stories that followed his resurrection. The contemporary newspaper reviews do not suggest that this disappointment was felt at the time, however, for although there was much speculation about the extent of Holmes's powers and some questioning as to whether he had reached his peak, the general tone of the reviews is one of satisfaction at the return of a familiar character who was so little changed. A close reading of stories like "The Adventure of the Dancing Men," "The Adventure of Charles Augustus Milverton," "The Adventure of the Six Napoleons," and "The Adventure of the Abbey Grange" will demonstrate that they are as good if not better than any of the earlier stories.

The thirteen stories, written in one batch, which appeared consecutively in the *Strand* from October 1903 to December 1904, and were reprinted in book form as *The Return of Sherlock Holmes* (1905), show a Holmes who is in full control of his substantial powers. He is still the only person who can appreciate the true significance of what he sees. He *is* the detective, the one who can understand, as Robert Louis Stevenson says, "the thousand eloquent clues, not of this mystery only, but of the countless mysteries by which we live surrounded."[10] The world that Holmes inhabits is still filled with objects that take on a special significance in his eyes only. Three wine glasses—two empty, one filled with sediment—and a half-empty bottle of wine lead to the solution of the murder in "The Adventure of the Abbey Grange." And just as Watson can deduce nothing from the hat in the earlier story "The Adventure of the Blue Carbuncle," so he can deduce nothing from the cut bell rope in "The Adventure of the Abbey Grange." Watson, who stands for the baffled reader of detective fiction, continues to have to be shown how to interpret the signs. On these occasions, by using his superior analytic ability as counterpoint to Watson's confusion, Holmes demonstrates that he is still the best reader of the signs, a master semiotician, as one contemporary approach to detective fiction would name him.[11]

The two comrades still remain cloistered in the snug world of

Baker Street, although the beginning of "The Adventure of the Golden Pince-Nez" illustrates their capacity to engage in separate activities while they sit together: Holmes is "deciphering the remains" of a medieval inscription, while Watson reads a "treatise upon surgery." Outside, true to form, "the wind howled down Baker Street while the rain beat fiercely against the windows" (CH, 2:607). The call to adventure is brought by a detective inspector: "What can he want?" Watson asks as the cab draws up at the door. "Want? He wants us. And we, my poor Watson, want overcoats and cravats and galoshes, and every aid that man ever invented to fight the weather" (CH, 2:608). The formula that served so well in the earlier series of stories is employed equally successfully after Sherlock Holmes's return, so the detective must, once again, go out in the threatening storm, travel through the familiar city, and brave a night that is both real and symbolic of all dangers that surround the champion of justice and order.

The Case Book of Sherlock Holmes

As the stories continued to be published—the next eight appeared in the *Strand* from September 1908 until September 1917 and in volume form entitled *His Last Bow;* the final twelve as *The Case Book of Sherlock Holmes*—various changes, reflective of the different conditions of the times and of Doyle's position as a successful writer and established family man, became evident. Doyle portrays a Holmes who becomes more polished, cultivated, social, and urbane as time goes by. As an initial indication of this trend, *The Hound of the Baskervilles* shows Holmes, on three separate occasions, putting aside the investigation in favor of the joys of culture; on the first occasion, he stops thinking in order to play his violin, on the second he takes Watson to an exhibition of paintings, and finally, in the incident that ends the novel, Holmes suggests to Watson that they stop for dinner before the evening's operatic entertainment, a performance of *Les Huguenots.* Later in the stories we find out that the earlier Holmes, who did not know or care about the Copernican theory, is now an expert linguist in an "ancient Cornish language" ("The Adventure of the Devil's Foot"); has written a monograph on polyphonic motets, "said by experts to be the last word upon the subject" ("The Adventure of the Bruce-Partington Plans"), and has done extensive research on Early English charters ("The Adventure of the Three Students").

Holmes's position as a cultivated man signals a similar change in his social skills, a change which alters his relationships with his clients and makes him a better detective. When he is patronized by the aristocracy ("The Adventure of the Priory School") or by a superior ("The Adventure of Thor Bridge"), Holmes remains calm and dignified. And when he deals with his inferiors, his new-found ability to be personable is made doubly evident when, somewhat to the reader's surprise, Watson assures us that "Sherlock Holmes was a past master in the art of putting a humble witness at his ease, and very soon, in the privacy of Godfrey Stevenson's abandoned room he had extracted all that the porter had to tell" ("The Adventure of the Missing Three-Quarter" [*CH*, 2:624]).

Doyle's personal elevation of Holmes is matched by a similar elevation in his approach to Holmes's work. The practical detective is now giving way to the omnipotent judge, the problem solver to the savior. In "The Adventure of Charles Augustus Milverton," Holmes actually turns criminal and persuades Watson to join him in an effort to burglarize Milverton's house. Excited by their new approach, Watson describes himself as "thrilled now with a keener zest than I had ever enjoyed when we were the defenders of the law instead of its defiers." Still, guided by their ideals ("The high object of our mission, the consciousness that it was unselfish and chivalrous" [*CH*, 2:578]), they do not have to worry about their position as lawbreakers; for them the ends fully justify the means.

Even when the situation deteriorates and the friends find themselves witnessing the murder of that "villainous character," Milverton, Holmes maintains his moral position as judge and jury. Refusing to let Watson, "spring out" to try to save the criminal, Holmes physically restrains his friend, who then explains to the reader: "I understood the whole argument of that firm restraining grip—that it was no affair of ours, that justice had overtaken a villain" (*CH*, 2:581). Holding to this position, Holmes will not help the police in their inquiries, and when he and Watson recognize the identity of the murderess from a photograph on display in a shop window, he enjoins silence once and for all by putting "his finger to his lips" as they turn away (*CH*, 2:582).

A later story, "The Adventure of the Missing Three-Quarter," shows Holmes—in light of his new position—redefining his relationship to the official police. He explains to Watson that he is an "irregular pioneer who goes in front of the regular forces of the country" (*CH,* 2:629). Implicit in this statement is Holmes's new position in regard to the police, a position which suggests that Holmes has a moral function that supersedes and is superior to the legal issues of any case. Justifying this position, he tells Watson: "I have the right to private judgment but he [Scotland Yard Officer Stanley Hopkins] has none. He must disclose all, or he is a traitor to his service" (*CH,* 2:647).

When Holmes has, on the basis of his private judgment, made a decision, he can, as in the case of Charles Augustus Milverton, allow justice to be dispensed or he can act as the judge and dispense justice himself. "The Adventure of the Abbey Grange" shows Holmes acting in this capacity while Watson stands for the jury. Captain Crocker has, in self-defense, killed Sir Eustace Brackenstall, a man who abuses his wife and is described as "a beast" and "a drunken hound." After weighing all the evidence, Holmes forms his own private judgment, allows Crocker to present his defense, and then sets up the sentencing. After announcing that it is "a great responsibility that I take upon myself," Holmes addresses the court: "Watson, you are a British jury, and I never met a man who was more eminently fitted to represent one. I am the judge. Now gentlemen of the jury, you have heard the evidence. Do you find the prisoner guilty or not guilty?" "Not guilty, my lord" said I. "Vox Populi, vox Dei. You are acquitted, Captain Crocker" (*CH,* 2:650).

In this manner, and in the general contempt with which Holmes regards Lestrade, Doyle declares that the official police and the legal system are so imperfect that they are incapable of dealing with moral issues. On the basis of Holmes's actions alone (although Doyle's letters at this time also reflect the same thing), it seems clear that Doyle was becoming more and more uneasy about the efficiency of the legal process and less and less hopeful that justice was being served. In criminal matters Doyle wants Holmes—as we have seen— to take the law into his own hands, while in socially delicate civil cases Holmes enforces his own idea of what is permissible. "So long as there is nothing criminal I am much more anxious to hush up private scandals than to give them publicity" (*CH,* 2:635) he tells us in "The Adventure of the Missing Three-Quarter." As the stories progress and the character of Holmes develops it becomes clear that Doyle has added a religious function to his character's secular role of detective; now Holmes is a saver of souls.

The Valley of Fear

The last of Doyle's full-length detective novels, written between the winter of 1913 and the spring of 1914, is set back in time to the end of the 1880s. *The Valley of Fear* is notable chiefly because it does more than provide Holmes with a "little problem" to alleviate the boredom of daily life. This adventure presents Holmes with a rare opportunity to come to grips with his nemesis, Professor Moriarty, one of the few arch-villains who dare to threaten the life of the detective. Holmes introduces Moriarty as, "the greatest schemer of all time, the organizer of every deviltry, the controlling brain of the underworld, a brain which might have made or marred the destiny of nations, that's the man!" (*CH*, 2:769) before he adds that his evil double, his "twin," is also the author of a book of "pure mathematics" so abstruse that there is no scientist in the world "capable of criticizing it" (*CH*, 2:770). Given his "phenomenal mathematical faculty" as evidence of his brilliant mind, Moriarty represents knowledge used in the service of evil. Moriarty is engaged in the devil's work and his singular talents turn him into a force that is almost omnipotent; he "pervades London," pulling strings and guiding evil from the center of a web of criminality that is enveloping the life of the city.

Like the serpent in the story of Adam and Eve, Moriarty represents knowledge used to promote the cause of evil, so his physical appearance is appropriately "reptilian"; "his face protrudes forward and is forever slowly oscillating from side to side." With his snake-like mannerisms, his brilliant mind, and his tremendous administrative ability, Moriarty is the arch-criminal who mirrors so exactly the arch-detective that the struggle between them can only be seen as the cosmic, Manichaean struggle of good versus evil.

The Valley of Fear is, like A Study In Scarlet, a split narrative; "The plot goes to America for at least half the book while it recounts the events which lead up to the crime in England."[12] The crime that Holmes and Watson are called in to solve is the (apparent) murder of a "remarkable man," John Douglas, who has been found shot in the head in the drawing room of his house. Doyle, who had boasted of what he described as "a real staggerer to the most confirmed reader," does surprise the reader by reintroducing a device that he had first used in "The Adventure of the Norwood Builder";

the murdered man is in fact not dead. John Douglas is in hiding, and the body, unrecognizable from extensive head wounds, is actually the body of an American enemy whom Douglas killed in self-defense. He then realized he could use the corpse as a ploy to escape from his enemies.

The explanation of Douglas's past is contained in the second section of the novel, a lengthy romantic-adventure saga entitled "The Scowrers," set in a coal-mining valley in the United States. Douglas, a Pinkerton agent in disguise, is sent to break up a menacing secret society known as the "Scowrers." After numerous near-misses, he does entrap most of the members before escaping from the valley with the local girl he loves.

The first section of the novel, set in England and called "The Tragedy of Birlstone," has been called "a very nearly perfect piece of detective-story writing"[13] by a critic who also suggests that the readers who don't like *The Valley of Fear* are motivated by their political objections to the conflict between the Scowrers and the people of the valley. The terrorist Scowrers are associated with the workers and trade unionism, and the elimination of the group is accomplished by a privately financed security agency, the Pinkertons, who work for the owners of the coal mines. Thus, the worker versus employer struggle is transformed so that the organized workers become vigilantes while the symbol of management repression, the Pinkerton agent, is the hero of the piece. This position on trade unionism is consistent with the rest of Doyle's views. He deplored the breaking of the bond that he believed existed in earlier times between master and servant, employer and employee, and he felt that this close relationship, destroyed by industrialism, had been degraded to such a point that the only thing that bound them was the cash nexus. Therefore, worker organizations were but one more example of a general decay.

The fact is that critics who dislike the plot can make a far more cogent argument against it on other grounds. The split narrative, like that in *A Study in Scarlet,* which juxtaposes, in separate narratives, the forms of the detective story and the romantic adventure story, is far less satisfying than the integrated detective story. The decision to get rid of Holmes, even as a listener, while the events that preceded the crime are encapsulated in what is—to all intents and purposes—a separate story, does not work. Furthermore, the absence of the comforting presence of Holmes is only underscored by the arrival of the younger, more physical Douglas who operates in a world of violence. In the usual world of Doyle's detective, the crime has been committed before Holmes and Watson arrive on the scene, and even though the crime is a violent one, Doyle does not have to describe it. In this novel, Doyle tries to show the violence first hand, and he is clearly uncomfortable with the material. The result of such tension is unconvincing melodrama.

Another reason why the adventure world seems alien—and this may be the primary reason why the split narrative fails—is that Doyle never seems in charge of his material when he writes about America. Too often the adventure story veers off into stilted melodrama, with stereotypical characters uttering clichéd phrases. When Doyle leaves the world of middle-class England, of what has become "his own fictional kingdom,"[14] he is not convincing. His United States is created out of anachronisms that come straight out of the boys' adventure stories that he read as a child. In spite of his own extensive travels in the U.S. and Canada, Doyle still feels fictionally most at home in a world that, to quote Mr. Podsnap, "gets up at eight, shaves close at a quarter past, breakfasts at nine, goes to the City at ten, comes home at half-past five and dines at seven."[15]

While not a convincing story, the American episode is interesting as an indication of Doyle's state of mind, for when the worlds of Holmes and the Scowrers—safe, homogenous England and violent, multi-ethnic America—are brought together under the watchful eye of the detective, it turns out that Holmes is not omniscient. The concluding section shows that in spite of all Holmes's precautions and warnings, the long arm of Moriarty can reach into the middle of the ocean where Douglas is found "accidentally" drowned. Instead of achieving closure by eliminating the criminal Moriarty from society, the story is left open-ended with Holmes stymied in his efforts and Moriarty at large. The hero of *The Valley of Fear,* the champion of all the virtues in the midst of corruption, is dead while the vicious Scowrers are triumphant. Further, the promise implicit in *The Hound of the Baskervilles,* that money made abroad could and should be returned to the mother country to restore her to her past glory, cannot be kept in *The Valley of Fear.* As in the previous novel, Douglas uses American money to renovate and maintain the piece of England that he inhabits, but he cannot stay there; he has to take his income and leave, for the danger posed by Moriarty is too great.

Seen in the context of a criminality out of control, of a chaos barely contained, it is not surprising that Holmes's ability to best Moriarty remains in doubt. The confrontation between the two has yet to take place; the outcome of the Manichaean struggle is postponed. The traditional ending to the Holmes story, the scene in which the triumphant two return to security to celebrate order, is replaced with a scene in which the detective, doubtful and anxious, can only hope for Moriarty's eventual destruction. Doyle can no longer create a character who can demonstrate the completion of his promise. "Barker beat his head with his clenched fist in his impotent anger. 'Do not tell me that we have to sit down under this? Do you say that no one can ever get back with this King devil?' 'No, I don't say that,' said Holmes, and his eyes seemed to be looking far into the future, 'I don't say that he can't be beat. But you must give me time—You must give me time!' We all sat in silence for some minutes while those fateful eyes still strained to pierce the veil" (*CH,* 2:866).

The ending of *The Valley of Fear* mirrors Doyle's concern about the world. By 1914 the world was at war, a war which, while optimistically titled "the war to end all wars," did only in fact give evidence of the bestial nature of man and demonstrate the endless difficulties of maintaining civilization in an era whose chief characteristics appeared to be militant nationalism and political self-interest. The writer who had created Holmes ten years previously in a more stable time no longer felt so sanguine about the state of society. Even Holmes, a character created to bring order out of chaos, could no longer ignore the pessimism and anguish generated by the events outside.

The conditions of society in the years 1913–1914 were so overwhelmingly dark, in Doyle's view, that he had to show them as penetrating the psyche of the world's most famous positivist rationalist. The confidence that had created Holmes, a character positive that the mysteries of the universe could be understood as long as the rules of rationalism and scientific experimentalism were followed, could not flourish in an age that demonstrated the futility of any such optimism. Doyle has Holmes make a promise, to Watson and to us, that he will remove the evil that is Moriarty, but his eyes, the eyes that previously could easily pierce the fog that surrounded him, are now "strained." And even though the reader knows in advance that in the final encounter between Holmes and Moriarty at the Reichenbach Falls, decency *is* triumphant, the sense of Holmes's frailty, his potential for failure in a world where the only certainty is that certainty no longer exists, remains.

His Last Bow

Only two of the remaining twelve short stories were set later than 1902, the date of Holmes's retirement to the Sussex downs to keep bees, and of these two—"His Last Bow" and "The Adventure of the Lion's Mane" (1926)—only the first is set in the period immediately before the war.[16] Written in 1917 for the *Strand*, "His Last Bow," takes place at nine o'clock on the evening of 2 August 1914, and, consonant with that time and day, it begins with an apocalyptic vision: "One might have thought already that God's curse hung heavy over a degenerate world, for there was an awesome hush and a feeling of vague expectancy in the sultry and stagnant air. The sun had long set, but one blood red gash like an open wound lay low in the distant west" (*CH*, 2:970). This passage, reminiscent of the start of *Sir Nigel*, when the purple cloud of the bubonic plague lay over England, is far from what Holmes readers had come to expect. "Degenerate" and "cursed" are words not usually associated with the familiar Victorian world of the detective. For most readers, Holmes epitomizes the last years of the nineteenth century, a time which, in the stories at least, has become a sort of urban golden age. "His Last Bow", with its background of the coming war and the advent of the twentieth century, displaces this image forever.

The mystery that Holmes has to solve has to do with uncovering a system of espionage set up by a German agent operating in England. The story is not at all complicated and Holmes's appearance and the capture of the master spy, Von Bork, is all but tangential to the real purpose of the story, which emerges in a discussion between the two Germans about the peculiar British idea of responsibility that the nation feels for her European neighbors. Van Bork's suggestion made to his arch-conspirator, Baron Von Herling, that Britain could not honorably abandon Belgium to the German invasion, is quickly refuted by the pragmatic German: "Tut, my dear sir, we live in a utilitarian age. Honour is a medieval conception" (*CH*, 2:972). Holmes, Watson, and the as yet unrealized actions of the British government give the lie to the German position and, in so doing, show the world that for Doyle, honor, far from being an outmoded concept, is an essential factor even in the modern world.

Holmes is not a hero for the twentieth century. The world he inhabits is a world that still uses and believes in words like "honor," "decency," and "fair play." The comment of one recent critic, "On occasion the stories echo contemporary anxieties, as in their fear of scandal, but in general they express the self-confidence of the period,"[17] is accurate only when speaking of the earlier stories. By the early twentieth century, the self-confidence of the nineteenth century had largely evaporated.

The impact of World War I on English society has been so widely documented elsewhere that it is unnecessary to detail the effects here, but Doyle's words, speaking of the period prior to the war, are indicative of a general feeling: "I can never forget, and our descendents can never imagine, the strange effect upon the mind which was produced by seeing the whole European fabric drifting to the edge of the abyss with absolute uncertainty as to what would happen when it toppled over" (*MA*, 323). Doyle's perception of a world out of control, of events gone so far that no amount of rational analysis could make order out of them, is inimical to the very concepts on which the Holmes stories are founded. The clairvoyant Holmes sees and announces in "His Last Bow" the demise of the world that he had once helped maintain: " 'There's an east wind coming, Watson.' 'I think not Holmes. It is very warm.' 'Good old Watson! You are the one fixed point in a changing age. There's an east wind coming all the same, such a wind as never blew on England yet . . . !' " (*CH*, 2:980). As this eulogy and the title suggest, "His Last Bow" should mark Holmes's last appearance. As it turned out, it was not the last Holmes story to be published, but it still stands as the effective end to this chapter and to the Holmes saga not only because "it records, metaphorically, Holmes's death,"[18] but also because it records the death of Edwardian England.

Chapter Six
The Scientific Romances

When Doyle began writing the first draft of his new novel *The Lost World* in 1911, scientific fiction as a genre was already well established. Jules Verne (1828–1905), who consciously developed a new type of story, is generally regarded as the father of modern science fiction, while H. G. Wells, who wrote science fiction stories some twenty years later, in the 1890s, is credited with having made an equally strong contribution.

Speaking of Wells's *First Men in the Moon* (1901), Verne, claiming scientific authenticity, explained: "I make use of physics. He invents. I go to the moon in a cannon ball, discharged from a cannon. Here there is no invention. He goes to Mars in an airship which he constructs of a metal which does away with the law of gravitation."[1] And Wells, in full agreement, said of Verne, "His work dealt almost always with actual possibilities of invention and discovery and he made some remarkable forecasts. . . . But these stories of mine do not pretend to deal with possible things: they are exercises of the imagination in a quite different field."[2]

Given Doyle's training as a doctor, his lifelong interest in scientific experimentation, plus a purely personal delight in inventions, it would seem that Doyle would be scientifically precise, and deal, like Jules Verne, in what is possible. But such is not the case. Doyle, like Wells, invents what he needs, although he makes very little use of scientific devices, and none of scientific terminology or explanations. Instead, it is more accurate to say that Doyle's stories use the atmosphere of science, or the trappings of science. Of course, some of his stories make use of an invention—the chairlike machine in "The Disintegration Machine"—or a scientific proposition—the color spectrum in *The Poison Belt,* for example—but in general, the emphasis in his writing is on the quest motif, not on science. Thus, unlike Jules Verne's work, Doyle's scientific tales make no claim to scientific veracity. Science is merely the peg on which the adventure hangs, leaving romance as the more descriptive term for Doyle's scientific romances.

One notable exception is a tale usually classified with his adventure stories, rather than with his scientific stories, in which Doyle does make use of contemporary scientific discoveries to prophesy the existence and use of certain inventions. Interestingly, "Danger" (1914) makes use of submarines, an invention that Verne had already introduced in his *Twenty Thousand Leagues under the Sea.* In Doyle's story a small European country armed with only eight submarines equipped with guns and torpedoes goes to war with an apparently invulnerable Great Britain. The small country wins because, as Doyle has the enemy captain John Sirius point out, if you use submarines "to attack merchant ships and avoid warships," you can stop all foodstuffs and supplies from getting to Britain.[3] In view of the fact that by 1917 the number of merchant vessels sunk by German submarines was steadily increasing every day, Doyle was indeed prescient—and technologically accurate—in some of his stories. But in what are the most important of his scientific tales, known as the Challenger stories and comprising the three novels, *The Lost World, The Poison Belt, The Land of Mist,* and the two short stories, "When the World Screamed" and "The Disintegration Machine," the emphasis is on adventure, rather than science.

The Lost World

For Doyle, *The Lost World* (1912) was the achievement of a long-held, much cherished, ambition. Some twenty years earlier, before he began to write *The White Company,* he had told his mother: "I have been thinking of trying a Rider Haggardy kind of book called *The Inca's Eye,* dedicated to all the bad boys of the Empire by one who sympathizes with them."[4] Doyle's story, *The Lost World,* is about a journalist, Edward Malone, who joins an eminent scientist, Professor Challenger, Professor Summerlee (Challenger's arch-rival), and the professional explorer Lord John Roxton in a journey to the upper Amazon to document the existence of a prehistoric "lost" world. The lost world motif had been explored by Rider Haggard in *King Solomon's Mines* (1895) so, in all other respects except for the title, this story is the novel that Doyle had wanted to write. It is, in the Rider Haggard tradition, a rousing imperialist adventure story written for boys, or as Doyle makes clear in his dedication to *The Lost World,* for the eternal boy in every adult: "I have wrought my simple plan, if I give one hour of joy to the boy who's half a man, or the man who's half a boy."[5] And, in a more grandiose moment: "My ambition is to do for the boy's book what Sherlock Holmes did for the detective tale."[6] Although Holmes's never-ending popularity makes such a wish almost impossible, *The Lost World*, with its magical journey, its group of ill-assorted but interesting adventurers, its lush topographical descriptions, its scenes of horror, and one of Doyle's best-loved and most memorable characters, Professor Challenger, all contribute to make this one of his best books. Even without Holmes, Professor Challenger should be enough to ensure Doyle's place among the best writers of scientific romances.

The dominant Professor Challenger, a character deliberately drawn in an exaggerated manner, is so energetic that he seems to overflow the pages. This is in fact literally true, for we meet Professor Challenger even before the book begins. The foreword, serving as introduction to the professor's contentious and quixotic nature, tells us that the narrator-author, Edward Malone, "desires to state that the injunction for restraint and the libel action have been withdrawn unreservedly by Professor G. E. Challenger."

Although Challenger is, apparently, larger than life, the novel's realistic beginning portrays a world infinitely small, bourgeois, and boring. On the first page, the narrator, Edward Malone, introduces us to a society where the middle class reigns supreme and respectability is all. Mr. Hungerton, "a fluffy, feathery, untidy, cockatoo; perfectly good-natured, but absolutely centered upon his own silly self" (*LW*, 3), represents the meaningless pretensions of this world. Malone is oblivious to this nonsense as he is courting Mr. Hungerton's daughter Gladys, a woman whose name, with all its respectable lower middle-class connotations, turns out to be more indicative of her true nature than her beautiful face. Like the traditional dark lady of fiction that her exotic beauty suggests, Gladys is a temptress and a betrayer, but, in a nice ironic twist on this fictional cliché, Gladys tempts men, not with illicit pleasure, but with gentility. Her passion is all spent in the service of Edwardian morality. Although she speaks the language of high adventure ("I want to be honoured by all the world as the inspirer of noble deeds" [*LW*, 8]), this speech is a parody, a parroting of words that no longer have any meaning. Gladys is no more a heroine than her father is a hero. Her real nature is revealed at the end of the book when Malone, returning from his "noble deed" and hoping to claim

Gladys as his bride, finds that she has already married a solicitor's clerk, "a vacuous, good-natured, scrubby, little man" (LW, 306). To add insult to injury, Gladys's former assertion, "I want a man of great deeds and strange experiences" (LW, 7), is belied when Malone finds out that her husband has never traveled further afield than the suburbs of London.

Initially Malone responds heroically to Gladys's words, but the actual call to adventure is issued by Professor Challenger in a scene that emphasizes the stultifying nature of contemporary British society, embodied here by the audience at a public scientific lecture. The audience, including some medical students who, in Doyle's view, presumably should know better, spend the evening deriding Challenger's findings and disparaging his work.

The confrontation between Challenger and the audience seems at first comic, especially when at the height of the fracas, the medical students, in response to Challenger's roar of "Who called me a liar?" hoist aloft a bespectacled "little" man: "Again the inoffensive one, plunging desperately was elevated high into the air" (LW, 80). However, in spite of the comic posture of the little man—of all the little men—the situation as Doyle sees it is a serious one. The contrast between the little man, made against his will an object of ridicule by the anonymous crowd, and the aggressive Challenger, standing on his own feet confronting his accuser is not one that Doyle intends us to ignore. In contrast to the birdlike man, Challenger is physically large, having "shoulders and a chest like a barrel—two enormous hands" and a "bellowing, roaring, rumbling voice" to match (LW, 26). Furthermore, in contrast to the circumscribed lives of the little men, Challenger is—as his name suggests—a law unto himself. Rude, unpredictable, and violent, he is beyond the reach of all bureaucratic rules and above all institutional regulations. Challenger is a character, "big in every way"[7] who cannot be contained, either by small rooms or by moribund ideas. Therefore, the call to adventure, nominally issued by Challenger to test his assertion that he has found, in the upper reaches of the Amazon, a "lost" world of prehistoric animals, is more than the traditional call to undertake a wondrous journey; in this book it is a call to take a stand against the stupidity and slackness of a mediocre society.

After the claustrophobic muddle of the suburban drawing room and meeting hall, Challenger is the proverbial breath of fresh air.

In fact, he is the antithesis of the middle class, a class whose petty strictures and emphasis on respectability make him furious. The men who inhabit that class—the petit bourgeois—provide the gray background against which Challenger's passions can be seen the more clearly. Challenger can be wrong, but he is not hypocritical, weak, or vacillating. Far from the familiar, calm, reasonable hero, Challenger is a furious, unreasonable hero, or more appropriately given the lack of heroism extant in bourgeois society, antihero. In an overly genteel world Challenger is a man notable for his lack of all restraint; he is not so much immoral as amoral.

In spite of the assertion of Malone's editor that "the big blank spaces in the map are all being filled in and there's no room for romance anywhere" (*LW*, 13), Challenger proves otherwise by conducting his party to a place in South America where, as a result of some freakish volcanic activity, "an area, perhaps as large as Sussex has been lifted up en bloc with all its living creatures" (*LW*, 52). Cut off from the rest of the continent, the plateau has kept various species of prehistoric animals, specifically those of the Mesozoic age, alive and well.

Once the men get onto the "lost" plateau, using a large felled tree as a bridge, Doyle develops "a fascinating dream-like atmosphere." The dream, "the most wonderful," as the explorers say, "that the imagination of man could conceive" (*LW*, 81), is one of primeval harmony, a harmony which continues for several chapters as the travelers move through "a verdant paradise of a thousand shades of green."[8] This Rousseauean vision of nature—one that, without the interference of man, exists in perfect balance—is full of wonderfully scented flowers, exotic birds, friendly "velvet" monkeys, and shady forest walks. Even the giant prehistoric animals sighted at a distance turn out to be gentle, herbivorous iguanodons.

This vision of natural harmony turns into a Darwinian nightmare, however, when they come upon a bare plain "strewn with boulders" that conceals a pit of the baby pterodactyls. These gargoyle-like birds born from "leathery, yellowish eggs" produced by "hideous mothers" are so terrifying that Doyle invokes the image of Dante's hell to help him describe the "crawling flapping mass of obscene reptilian life" that fills the rookery (*LW*, 166–67). Standing sentry to this ghastly birthplace are the full-grown male pterodactyls, figures from a particularly terrifying hallucination: "tall, grey and withered, more like dead and dried specimens than actual living creatures, sat the horrible males, absolutely motionless save for the rolling of their red eyes or an occasional slap of their rat-trap beaks as a dragon fly went past. Their huge membranous wings were closed by folding their forearms, so that they sat like gigantic old women, wrapped in hideous web-coloured shawls, and with their ferocious heads protruding above them" (*LW, 167*). As this lengthy passage shows, Doyle's ability as an imaginative horror writer is second to none. These scenes of terror, filled with devil imagery and the atmosphere of Gothic nightmares, and so beautifully contrasted with the pastoral verdancy of the earlier passages, are masterpieces of the horror-story genre.

The evil vision of the flesh-eating birds marks the beginning of a series of terrifying encounters, culminating in a nighttime encounter between Malone and a carnivorous dinosaur. The adventurers first see the dinosaur when they are all together by the campfire, striking them as "a vision of a horrible mask, like a giant toad's, of a warty leprous skin and of a loose mouth all beslobbered with fresh blood" (*LW, 178*). That night, with the help of a firebrand, the friends manage to drive off the beast, but, as in all nightmares, the true facing of the terror has to take place in the dark and on an individual basis. Thus, the next night Malone, returning from a solitary reconnaissance, finds that the beast, which has apparently been tracking him all day, is now running silently after him through the dark forest: "With my knees shaking beneath me, I stood and glared with starting eyes down the moonlit path which lay behind me. All was quiet as in a dream landscape. Silver clearings and the black patches of the bushes—nothing else could I see. Then from out of the silence, imminent and threatening, there came once more that low throaty croaking, far louder and closer than before" (*LW, 207*).

Malone escapes but further investigation of the plateau makes it clear that his struggle with the dinosaur was but an illustration of what life is like all over the lost world. In fact, the explorers find themselves in the middle of a vivid demonstration of the struggle for survival, a microcosm of Darwin's theory as to the adaptability of the species, dramatically enacted before their eyes. To complete the history lesson, they find out that there are humans on the plateau and that the land is divided between two warring groups: the fearsome ape-men (apparently the missing link in the evolutionary chain), who are the more powerful, and the Accala Indians: "little, clean

limbed, red fellows whose skin glowed like polished bronze" (*LW,*
231), who have been marooned on the plateau since it was severed
from the mainland.

By virtue of its unique position, the lost world has compressed
time, so that the ape-men and their modern successors are brought
face to face to battle for their respective place in history in a drama
re-creating events which took place "at the dawn of human history."[9]
The physically small Indians armed only with spears and bows and
arrows are, in this instance, aided by the four modern men equipped
with rifles and bullets. The cruel ape-men are thus soundly defeated
in one of the decisive battles of the evolution of man. In a scene in
which Doyle rather naively emphasizes the superiority of the tall
white men, the explorers are shown truly making history.

Yet even though the ape-men have been—and must be—defeated, Doyle does not approve of the fact that the end of this
particular evolutionary chain leads to Mr. Hungerton. Professor
Challenger, who at one point had been found to have an uncanny
physical resemblance to the king of the ape-men ("they might have
been kinsmen" [*LW,* 222]), is the pattern of a man needed at the
beginning of the twentieth century. The ape-men must be beaten
in the Mesozoic age, Doyle is saying, but modern men could use
an infusion of their spirit; a spirit exemplified by the professor who
combines the aggression of the ape-men with the mind of a brilliant
scientist: "Only above the eyebrows, where the sloping forehead and
low curved skull of the ape-men were in sharp contrast to the broad
brow and magnificent cranium of the European, could one see any
marked difference (*LW,* 232). By combining these qualities, Challenger is the best of pre-historic man and the best of modern man—
a signal indication to the little men of what is possible. Also, of
course, this combination means that Challenger is the man for all
seasons; he is fit for both physical and mental adventures.

In his presentation of Challenger as the role model for the Mr.
Hungertons of the world, Doyle is not advocating a return to the
bestiality of the ape-men. Rather, he is suggesting that as life in a
postindustrial, materialistic society has led to a spiritual and moral
decline, a salutary look at a time when people had to fight to survive
and life was worth fighting for would not come amiss. Challenger,
the ape-man/scientist, is a perpetual reminder of qualities that the
middle class has forgotten ever existed.

The concluding scene—when the friends have escaped and returned in triumph to London—reemphasizes the lesson from the past that the friends had witnessed. Again, in a replay of the first scene, there is the comic chaos of the disbelieving audience, and again Challenger explains and expostulates, but this time Challenger carries his evidence with him and gives it in the form of a terrible warning. As the audience demands visible proof of the adventure, Challenger, calling, "Come my pretty, my pretty," coaxes a horrible baby pterodactyl out of its box to remind the audience of "the devil of our childhood in person" (LW, 299). Challenger's revenge is attended, of course, with a certain degree of relish. The carnivorous gargoyle-like bird is the perfect way for Challenger—and Doyle—to shake people out of their complacency. But the real lesson of the pterodactyl is that he comes from a time when, in the struggle for existence, the meek and unadventurous did not survive. Challenger, with his ability to live in both worlds, brings the pterodactyl to urban London as a warning that should such a time come again, the species of little men would be quickly extinguished. Only by learning to be more like Challenger can they hope to ensure their continuance.

Unfortunately for the female characters in The Lost World—and for Doyle's female readers, women in this novel seem to be permanently identified with the world of the little men. Gladys Hungerton, the dark lady of the romance, is shown to be nothing more than the quintessential suburban housewife, the "little" woman fit for the "little" man, but the other female character, Challenger's own wife, of whom more might be expected, also turns out to be nothing but a fussy "enraged chicken."

In what at first appears to be a completely gratuitous incident the reader is introduced to Challenger's wife when the professor, quite literally, picks her up and puts her on a "high pedestal of black marble" (LW, 34) to stem her fussing. Malone, witnessing the scene, reports that "a more absurd object than she presented cocked up there with her face convulsed with anger, her feet dangling, her body rigid for fear of upset, I could not imagine" (LW, 34). Leaving aside the comedic and ironic aspects of this act, the underlying message seems quite clear: these women are at least equal participants in (and, perhaps, given their position as moral arbiters of society, the prime exponents of) a society that has replaced adventure with superficial social restrictions, curiosity with fear, and aggression with meekness.

Whatever the reason, there is no question that the "little" men have become too domesticated and too feminine for the world of adventure Doyle admires. The incident with Challenger's wife is, therefore, an important one. Challenger, the rebellious man-boy, is not to be nagged by his wife, is not to be told what to do, is not to be domesticated in any way. By using his superior physical strength to remove the irritant, he shows how women, and presumably their all-too-pervasive femininity, can simply be put aside. Challenger's action epitomizes the idea—which in American literature is vividly expressed by the Huck Finn fantasy—of overt boyish disobedience to maternal female authority. The flagrancy of Challenger's move in picking his wife up and depositing her on a pillar indicates the extent of the frustration felt by Doyle's adventurous men at what is, from their perspective, the smallness of a world represented by women. It is only without female entanglements that the four standard bearers of adventure can light out for the unexplored places on the map.

The subject matter of *The Lost World* is often thought to have been engendered by certain events in Doyle's life. In 1909, for example, Doyle had had a British Museum scientist come to Sussex to take plaster casts of fossils, like "huge lizard's tracks"[10] found in a nearby quarry, and he noted in his autobiography that on a trip taken that same year he saw a strange animal "like a young ichthyosaurus" on a Greek island. This period also saw him become friends with the famous zoologist, Sir Edwin Ray Lankester,[11] to whom a reference appears in *The Lost World.*

But while these incidents are no doubt enlightening as indications of Doyle's interest in paleontology, the key to this novel lies in the energy and excitement embodied in the character of Professor Challenger. The writer's imagination seems to have been ignited more by Challenger than by any other character, except possibly Sir Nigel. Doyle's very real affection for Challenger can be seen in the photograph he had taken of himself dressed up to resemble Challenger complete with false beard, adhesive eyebrows, and a wig. He was so enamored of this disguise (and presumably of his ability to *be* Challenger) that he seriously tried to talk the editor of the *Strand* into using this photograph as an illustration for *The Lost World* when it was serialized in the magazine.[12] To his surprise, the editor, who refused Doyle's request, then had to argue Doyle out of this notion. Clearly, Doyle's fictional construct had become his alter ego, the embodiment of many of his male fantasies.

It seems apparent that the more constrained Doyle felt, the more he was drawn to Challenger's ability to act. In large part, action negates the sense, so prevalent in the Holmes stories of this time and in much of Doyle's personal correspondence, of a world closing in. Challenger's energy comes from his creator's delight in being able to vicariously break all laws and disregard every rule. The famous writer and established family man with serious literary and social responsibilities uses Challenger to rejuvenate his old sense of zest and enthusiasm for all the variations of life. The excitement in the story is directly attributable to Doyle's having found a way to inhabit a carefree world once more. If *The Lost World* appeals to the "boy" in all his readers, it is in large part because the boy in Doyle was transferred so successfully to Challenger.

The Poison Belt

Four months after the final installment of *The Lost World* was published in the *Strand* magazine in November 1912, Professor Challenger made his second appearance, in *The Poison Belt* (1913). This novel begins as the four friends, Challenger, Summerlee, Roxton, and Malone, gather to celebrate the third anniversary of their "lost" world adventure. The celebration, however, cannot take place given the event, "which is unique in all human annals" that is about to begin. [13] This event, signaled by a terse telegram from Challenger, "Bring oxygen," is nothing less than the end of the world, brought on by the belt of poisonous ether (the element through which Doyle tells us the planets move) that is slowly enveloping the planet and killing all forms of life. Based on international newspaper reports of unusual human activity, as well as his own observations of cosmic disturbances in the color spectrum, Challenger foresees this disaster and determines to witness, for as long as possible, the end of his world. The oxygen that he has commandeered is to be used to keep the five people (the four men plus the redoubtable Mrs. Challenger) alive in a sealed room specifically prepared as their last refuge.

While the rest of the world, totally unprepared, is paralyzed and killed by the poisonous ether, the five friends live for one final day and night. (A true romantic, Malone reminds himself that they have "one last sunset," one "final" sunrise, before their oxygen supply gives out.) However, just when their oxygen fails and Challenger, using resounding biblical language ("Into the hands of the Power that made us we render ourselves again!" [*PB*, 101]), heroically speeds them on their way by breaking a window, the belt of ether is found to have passed, leaving them alive. Furthermore, as the friends return from their first outing to the "dead" city of London, they are greeted by people awakening from a trancelike state; golfers continue to golf, postmen to deliver letters, and horses to pull carts up hills. The effects of the deadly ether are only temporary, and the world wakes up exactly as though nothing had happened.

This gentle reawakening is completely at odds with the scenes of death and destruction associated with the events of the previous night: the train full of "dead" passengers that crashed into another train stalled in the middle of the tracks; the fires started from all the untended hearths and stoves, one of which led to all of Brighton being "aflame by nightfall" (*PB*, 99). But *The Poison Belt* is a fable that uses a scientific accident to underscore what is a moral and spiritual warning: mankind, grateful to be alive, must learn to be humble. In terms of the plot, Doyle tells us that the glimpse of what-might-have-been is sufficient to change the world's behavior. As the *Times* notes, "Solemnity and humility are at the base of our emotions today. May they be the foundations upon which a more earnest and reverent race may build a more worthy temple" (*PB*, 145). This editorial also speaks for the author of the warning tale: by showing *us* a glimpse of what might be, he hopes that, like the chastened inhabitants of his fictional world, his readers will be similarly awakened and made humble.

The Poison Belt is not one of Doyle's more satisfactory stories, but it does bring to light many of the philosophic concerns that he was struggling to resolve. At some point in the ten years preceding the writing of this story, Doyle had become seriously interested in Spiritualism, or psychical research as he preferred it to be called. And sometime in the following two or three years, when he was "satisfied with the evidence," he announced that he himself had become a Spiritualist.[14] It is not clear from his letters or his autobiography exactly when he reached that point, nor is it necessary for us to pinpoint the exact moment. What is clear is that *The Poison Belt* reflects many of the contradictions and fears that were to find a resolution in Spiritualism. Many of these spiritual issues were to be discussed later and in greater depth in the books, pamphlets,

and articles that Doyle devoted to Spiritualism, but *The Poison Belt*—
read as a morality tale—is a good initial indication of where his
philosophic and religious concerns were leading him.

The Land of Mist

If *The Poison Belt* suggests Doyle's potential involvement with
Spiritualism, *The Land of Mist* (1925), written eleven years later in
the period between the first and second world wars, proclaims it
openly. In the time in between Doyle had devoted himself to the
Spiritualists, and this didactic novel, almost an apologia for the
cause, bears witness to the strength of his belief. His fervent commitment to the ideas propagated by the Society for Psychical Research was brought about by the kind of changes that he saw taking
place in postwar Britain, changes which fueled his deepening belief
that the world as he had known it was irrevocably destroyed. While
many other writers responded to what has been termed the "Age
of Disillusion" with the use of irony, satire, and black humor,
Doyle's response was to find a system that gave him a renewed sense
of optimism and hope. *The Poison Belt,* written in 1913, when there
was still some hope of averting a full-scale war, contains Doyle's
warning to the world that it cannot go on as usual. *The Land of
Mist,* written in 1924, when World War I, which left eight million
dead, was seen as only the prelude to a greater confrontation, contains Doyle's description of the new and better world that he had
found.

The Land of Mist, with its 1920s setting, immediately places the
reader in the postwar world. The once ever-youthful journalist,
Edward Malone, is a changed man, on whom "post-war conditions
and new world problems had left their mark," while the once ram-
bunctious Professor Challenger, suffering from the death of his wife,
is a man who would "have gone down" had it not been for the care
and support of his daughter, Enid. [15] The postwar Challenger is now
only a subdued version of his former self. Furthermore, where once
he was an energetic anarchist, he is now the defender of the status
quo. The revolutionary theory that Doyle is concerned with here is
that life as we know it is only a small part of the spirit's journey
to fulfillment and that when the spirit moves on, it can commu-
nicate, by means of certain "mediums" who are sympathetic to the
spirit world, with the living. Given the act of faith that the accep-

tance of such an idea entails, Challenger, the man of science, remains skeptical, arguing when asked about the many intelligent men who have taken up Spiritualism: "Every great mind has its weaker side. It is a sort of reaction against all the good sense. You come suddenly upon a vein of nonsense" (*LM*, 16).

Of course, given Doyle's proselytizing purpose, it is clear that Challenger will eventually change his mind in the face of the mounting evidence: first, a clairvoyant describes a spirit emanation that turns out to be their "dead" colleague, Professor Summerlee; then, at a séance attended by Enid and Malone, Malone talks to an emanation of his dead mother ("a little, squat, dark figure which waved its hands in joy when he spoke to it" [*LM* 97]); and Lord John Roxton, having returned from climbing Everest to look for another kind of adventure, joins forces with Malone. By now, everyone except the arch-skeptic is convinced. Finally in a culminating scene, Challenger goes forth to battle the forces of ignorance only to become an adherent when he is given some heretofore secret information about the deaths of two of his friends, deaths for which he had—mistakenly—felt responsible.

Challenger is convinced by the evidence just as Doyle expects to convince his readers with his evidence, given in the extensive appendix, which verifies most of the important experiences of English Spiritualism. As the friends join up to set out on their last adventure, the quest for the advancement of psychic research, Doyle makes a promise to them and to us: "a future which had ceased to be bounded by the narrow horizon of death and which now stretched away into the infinite possibilities and development of continued survival of personality, character and work" (*LM*, 276).

In a more detailed exposition of the earlier anxiety expressed in *The Poison Belt*, Doyle now attributes the world's downward slide to materialism and capitalistic notions of progress, which have hindered the quest for "spiritual progress" (the heroic language is entirely appropriate to Doyle's view). World War I, Doyle explains, was the watershed in this decline; for those four years of war were so terrible that they could only be explained as a warning to us to follow Christ's teachings more closely. During the six years after the war, Doyle became increasingly sure that this warning was going unheeded. In an effort to place the blame where he feels it belongs he names each country specifically: "Russia became a cesspool. Germany was unrepentant of her terrible materialism which had been the prime cause of the war. Britain was confused and distracted, full of wooden sects which had nothing of life in them" (*LM*, 35). Having given the indictment, he warns the transgressors that this state of affairs cannot continue: "All have sinned and their punishment will be in exact proportion" (*LM*, 36).

The Land of Mist details a further change in Doyle's beliefs, this time in his attitude to science. In this story and for the first time in his life he insists that science is culpable for our obsession with materialism. Speaking on behalf of the Spiritualists, Mr. Mailey asserts: "It is this scientific world which is at the bottom of much of our materialism. It has usually been a curse to us, for it has called itself progress, whereas we are really drifting very steadily backwards" (*LM*. 57). Mailey's strong language, reiterated by other Spiritualists throughout the book, serves to underscore what was, by now, Doyle's complete rejection of science. All his life the writer had felt that science represented a way for the betterment of mankind but now, apparently so disgusted by the uses that science had been put to in the war, he turned against what had been one of his sustaining beliefs.[16] From this point on, Doyle believed that to embrace science was to embrace the cause of mechanized violence.

Unfortunately, as Campbell puts it, Doyle's proselytizing purpose "breaks down the distinctions between a work of imagination and a religious tract."[17] The author constantly breaks into the plot to lecture the reader on spiritualist theory or history, while other parts of the plot are subverted to dramatize Doyle's didactic points. For example, in order to illustrate his contention that Christianity has failed to help people, Doyle abruptly introduces a gratuitous story of two small children who are beaten by their alcoholic father and starved by their vicious stepmother. Just when the brother and sister are facing certain death at the hands of their brutal father, their gentle, loving "dead" mother appears to them and, in a blaze of light, guides them to the home of a lonely, childless Spiritualist "who was summoned suddenly to the door and found two little apologetic figures outside it" (*LM*, 195). To ensure that justice is served, the father, in a drunken stupor, falls down an open coalhole and dies in agony.

In another section, the writer's need to demonstrate the universality of Spiritualism takes the form of a séance where the spirits exemplify different races, ages, and creeds. The first is a black child, unhappily called Wee One, who delivers his messages from the other world in clichéd baby talk: "I do my job as eight-year child.

When job done then Wee One become Big One all in one day"
(*LM,* 65). The second is a well-educated Englishman, the third an
unintelligible, unnamed Catholic soul from "the lower depths," and
the fourth an American Indian, named Red Cloud, who speaks like
a character from a simplified version of a story in the *Boy's Own
Paper:* "How the squaw? How the papooses? Strange faces in the
wigwam tonight" (*LM,* 71).

Despite the shortcomings—and there are many—of *The Land of
Mist* as a story, its importance to Doyle cannot be overestimated.
By combining the subject of psychic research with the novel form,
he hoped to convince his many readers of fiction of the truth about
Spiritualism. The novel did sell a respectable 38,000 copies in five
years, but there is no indication that the cause of Spiritualism fared
better as a result. For Doyle, though, the writing of this religious
tract was of the utmost importance; "Thank God," he said to his
editor, Greenhough Smith, when the manuscript was completed,
"that book is done! It was to me so important that I feared I might
pass away before it was finished."[18]

"When the World Screamed"

Fortunately for his non-Spiritualist admirers, Doyle next wrote
two Challenger stories that did not proselytize for the cause of
psychic research. And, freed in these stories from the burden of
Doyle's beliefs, Challenger resumes his old energy, his arrogance,
and his interest for the reader.

The first of these, "When the World Screamed," published in
the *Strand* magazine in 1928, is the story of Challenger's attempt
to use technology to pierce to the core of the earth. Returning to
the revolutionary scientific speculations that he had abandoned in
The Land of Mist, the professor asserts that the center of the earth
is living epiderm because "the world upon which we live is itself a
living organism, endowed as I believe, with a circulation, a respi-
ration, and a nervous system of its own" (*BSF,* 171). As the story
opens, the professor's assertion is about to be tested; Challenger has
dug down eight miles beneath the earth's surface where he has
positioned a special brace to hold the mechanized electrical boring
device that will penetrate the earth's living center.

Challenger, speaking to the artesian engineer whose help he needs,
shows that he is as rude and overbearing as he ever was: "You are

probably aware, sir, since Council schools are now compulsory that the Earth is flattened at the Poles" ("BSF," 171), but in the matter of taking liberties with Mother Nature, Challenger has gone too far. As the rod is "shot into the nerve ganglion of Old Mother Earth," the earth, emitting a hideous howl, first sends up a spume of a "vile and treacly substance" and then, in a volcanic convulsion, spits out all the machinery lodged beneath the crust before burying the pit "from human sight forever" ("BSF," 189). Nature is thus able to reject emphatically the professor's effrontery.

Clearly, Challenger's experiment in this story is as Waugh and Greenberg suggest, "little more than a rape."[19] The earth is female, the engineers and scientist male. The earth "shivers and trembles," has "palpitations" and "throbs" all during the time that the engineers "sink a shaft," use "tools," and "penetrate to the core." While it is easy to smile at the story's structure and Doyle's choice of words, we should not allow a post-Freudian reading to obscure a deeper level of meaning. Challenger's experiment is to demonstrate that the world has feelings. The conclusion of his experiment shows not only that it does but that there are certain indignities, certain trespasses, that the feeling earth will not tolerate. Doyle's story suggests that we should be more appreciative of a bountiful earth, more careful of our actions, some of which violate the earth's integrity, and more cautious in our pursuit of its treasures.

"When the World Screamed" is an antiscientific story in which Challenger is rebuked along with all the reckless empire builders who have not yet learned to be humble. As the enfant terrible that he so clearly is, Challenger *has* managed, as he boasts, to "set the whole world screaming," but the story suggests that in return the world has finally taught him respect for something other than himself.

"The Disintegration Machine"

This story, which appeared in the *Strand* magazine in 1929, is the final one featuring Professor Challenger. And Doyle uses this opportunity to deal with a concern that he did not think he had made manifest previously: his great fear of the evil possibilities of science. In "The Disintegration Machine," his belief that science is largely immoral is expressed directly by the inventor Nemor, a man whose behavior is so terrible that it can only be controlled by a character who, like Holmes in the later stories, is not afraid to mete out the appropriate brand of justice.

Actually, in this story Challenger is very like the arch-detective and "The Disintegration Machine" very like a detective story. The opening scene shows Malone's editor, Mr. McArdle, asking Challenger to look into a case of what appears to be scientific hyperbole; a machine has been invented which can dissolve matter into infinitesimal particles. This serious claim has to be submitted to a qualified judge and, as Malone points out to Challenger, "He [McArdle] has turned to you again and again when he needed the highest qualities in some investigation. That is the case now" (*BSF*, 155). Having thus established Challenger's past achievements as an investigator of scientific problems, Malone ensures Challenger's participation on this case when he tells him that the inventor, Nemor, is eager to sell his machine as a weapon to the highest bidder, Russia. To investigate a scientific "miracle" and to save the world is a task well worthy of Challenger's time and so, using a Holmesian phrase to signal his agreement, "Malone, I am at your service" ("DM," 156), they set off for Enmore Gardens to see for themselves.

The mad scientist, Theodore Nemor, in familiar villainous guise, is a divided personality; "Up to his forehead he is unformed; His large soft face was like an underdone dumpling of the same colour and moist consistency," but from his eyebrows up "there was a splendid cranial arch." The personification of the corruption of science, the lower Nemor is a "vile crawling conspirator," the upper "a great thinker and philosopher" ("BSF," 151).

The disintegration machine, which is described like the chair used by the time traveler in H. G. Wells's *The Time Machine,* does indeed work as Malone and Challenger prove in two separate experiments. Once this fact is proved, and once it becomes evident that Nemor will sell his machine to the Russians, Challenger assumes the role of judge, jury, and executioner. Having learned which position of the lever assures the disintegration of matter, Challenger tricks Nemor into sitting in the chair and summarily executes him by dissolving all his particles. Nemor is no more.

Challenger is so sure of his moral position that he is able to justify it immediately and calmly to Malone: "The interesting personality of Mr. Theodore Nemor has distributed itself throughout the cosmos, his machine is worthless, and a certain foreign Government has been deprived of knowledge by which much harm might have been wrought. Not a bad morning's work, young Malone" ("BSF," 164). As Malone continues to protest, Challenger silences him with

much the same argument that Holmes used with Watson: " 'The
first duty of a law-abiding citizen is to prevent murder,' said Challenger. 'I have done so. Enough, Malone, enough! The theme will
not bear discussion' " ("BSF," 165). Thus Challenger the investigator, like Holmes the investigator, becomes the judge of public
morality and the "guardian of the status quo."[20] The arch-scientist
acts to preserve the order of England against a misuse of science.

Chapter Seven
The Nonfiction

The Victorians were almost as familiar with Doyle in his character of public activist, as they were with the character of Sherlock Holmes. Candidate for political office (he was defeated when he ran for Parliament in 1902 and in 1906), military historian, inventor, detective, war correspondent, explorer, and sportsman, Doyle appeared capable of doing everything and doing it all well. As a writer and a man who felt passionately committed to whatever he was engaged in, he wrote extensively about his various experiences both in unpublished letters to friends and family and in published letters, essays, and pamphlets.

Doyle as Detective

Almost from the very first appearance of Sherlock Holmes, the public identified the author with his creation. To Doyle's chagrin, letters from all over the world begging the great detective for help were delivered without comment and without delay to Arthur Conan Doyle. And although Doyle usually declined to interest himself or his character in any real-life mysteries, in one or two cases he nevertheless ventured an opinion. In the case of the mysterious disappearance of a young woman's fiancée, Doyle was able to reconstruct the flight of the young man and, "by a . . . process of deduction, to show her very clearly whither he had gone and how unworthy he was of her affections."[1] Although Doyle maintained strict secrecy about the details of the case, the abandoned woman's last letter testifies to the accuracy of his analysis: "As you say, I have had an extraordinary escape and I hate to think of what might have happened if he hadn't gone away when he did."[2] Then there were the two cases that made Doyle famous as a detective in his own right, when he undertook to overturn the convictions of two men who had already been arrested and imprisoned.

The Edalji case. Briefly, the facts as presented to Doyle were these: George Edalji, the son of a local vicar who happened to be a Hindu, was accused, convicted, and sentenced for a series of animal mutilations that had occurred over a period of some months in the neighborhood of his village, Great Wyrley, in Staffordshire. Lacking any convincing evidence, the police, apparently motivated by racial prejudice, took Edalji into custody. In spite of the fact that Edalji had an alibi for the night of the most vicious attack, had been a brilliant student all his life, was now an established practitioner of the law, and possessed an impeccable character, the police successfully prosecuted Edalji, who was then sentenced to several years' hard labor.

Although Edalji had already served three years of his sentence when Doyle first became aware of the case, after reviewing the evidence presented by the police, Doyle did not hesitate. As he put it, "I realized that I was in the presence of an appalling tragedy, and that I was called upon to do what I could to set it right" (*MA*, 210). He immediately set out to reconstruct the case by visiting Great Wyrley and interviewing all the participants, and in a piece of detective work reminiscent of Holmes, Doyle was able to collect enough evidence to demolish the case in a matter of weeks. He then put the accumulated evidence before the public in a series of articles published in the *Daily Telegraph* beginning in January 1907. The articles—and Doyle's speeches on the same subject—were followed by a huge outpouring of public sympathy for George Edalji.

Largely due to Doyle's relentless efforts to keep the case before the public, a commission was set up to reinvestigate the affair. The prisoner was finally freed, but as the commission would not go so far as to recommend any compensation or public apology of any kind, Doyle continued to feel that justice had been denied to George Edalji: "To this day," he wrote in his autobiography, "this unfortunate man, whose humble family has paid many hundreds of pounds in expenses, has never been able to get one shilling of compensation for the wrong done. It is a blot upon the record of English Justice, and even now it should be wiped out. What a travesty of Justice!" (*MA*, 212–13).

The Slater case.   In another case involving a travesty of justice Doyle undertook to do for Oscar Slater what he had done for Edalji: "I went into the matter most reluctantly, but when I glanced at the facts, I saw that it was an even worse case than the Edalji one, and that this unhappy man had in all probability no more to do

with the murder for which he had been condemned that I had"
(*MA,* 216).

Doyle did not feel for Slater the same kind of personal affinity
that had drawn him to Edalji, but he did not allow this to make
any difference in a case where the man "was poor and friendless"
and "the public had lost its head and so had the police" (*MA,* 217).
While Doyle was able to tear apart the official case against Slater,
he was not able to suggest a solution to the mystery of who did
murder the elderly Miss Gilchrist while her maid was out buying
the evening paper. What Doyle *was* able to do was "start a newspaper
agitation" (*MA,* 218) and to write a pamphlet, *The Case of Oscar
Slater* (1912), which was largely responsible for the formation of a
new commission of inquiry. Doyle's pamphlet carefully sets out the
evidence presented by the police as damning to Slater before the
author, with equal care, demolishes it: "It is impossible to read and
weigh the facts without feeling deeply dissatisfied with the pro-
ceedings, and morally certain that justice was not done."[3] He uses
this opportunity to suggest new lines of inquiry to the prosecutors,
arguing, for instance, that the theft of the brooch may have been
just a cover-up for a more serious theft. And, in conclusion, he
asserts that, as the murderer was apparently admitted by Miss
Gilchrist or had a key to her flat, the police had better look much
closer to home for her assailant.

In spite of Doyle's book and to his continuing dismay, Oscar
Slater remained in prison serving a life sentence of hard labor for
the next eleven years. In 1925 Doyle committed himself to try
again, and after numerous letters to members of Parliament and the
press, he persuaded a Glasgow journalist, William Park, to write
a new account of the case, *The Truth About Oscar Slater,* which was
published in 1927. Doyle wrote the introduction to Park's book,
reiterating the points about official incompetence that he had made
previously in his own pamphlet. Doyle's persistence had its reward
when a long overdue pardon was finally granted the same year.
Slater was pardoned, but, like Edalji, he was not vindicated.

After all that time, nothing would now satisfy Doyle but a public
proclamation of Slater's innocence, and so once again he began his
letter-writing campaign to the newspapers and to Parliament. Slater
was freed in November 1927, and in June 1928, after a new trial
had been held and a full review of all the evidence made public,

Slater was finally declared innocent. Although Doyle was jubilant at the belated vindication of Slater, the whole affair left him saddened and cynical, exclaiming: "What a story! What a scandal! . . . What a cesspool it all is."[4]

The Crime of the Congo. In his attack on another "cesspool," this time an international one, Doyle displayed the same spirit of knight-errantry that had prompted him to fight for Edalji and Slater. The case of the appalling treatment of the African natives who, since 1884, had lived under Belgian rule in what had been named, ironically it appeared, the Congo Free State, needed no detective work on Doyle's part; the facts had already been made public in the evidence presented by the British Consul at Boma, Roger Casement, to the British House of Commons in 1903. As a result of this presentation, the Belgian king had promised to reform the methods by which the natives were forced to produce large quantities of the ivory and rubber comprising the riches of the Free State. But by 1908, this promise still had not been kept. The natives did not need a detective; they needed a champion. Doyle, "deeply moved" by "the wrongs of these unhappy and helpless negroes" (*MA,* 229), was such a man.

After sorting through and reviewing all the published evidence, Doyle joined forces with Roger Casement, E. D. Morel, and the Congo Reform Association. Convinced that the general public would be outraged once the story was thoroughly disclosed, Doyle turned to his best weapon—his writing—to publicize the details of the brutal oppression. *The Crime of the Congo,* published in 1909, is, as Doyle claims, "a general account which would cover the whole field and bring the matter up to date."[5]

This short report, published in pamphlet form and dedicated to E. D. Morel, "the Unselfish Champion of the Congo races in token of sincere admiration for his long and heroic fight," is a carefully documented compendium of verified facts and figures interspersed with some eye-witness accounts of the floggings, rapes, and murders of which the Belgians stood accused. The shock value of these accounts is intensified by a series of photographs at the beginning of the book showing natives who had been mutilated by their Belgian masters. *The Crime of the Congo* moves from a summary of the early history of the white man's involvement in the Congo in a section called "How the Congo Free State came to be founded," through the development of the highly structured rubber and ivory producing company, the International Association of the Congo, as a mechanism for administering the territory, to the testimony of various people—administrators, agents, missionaries, teachers—who worked in the Congo, and finally to the testimony of the abused natives themselves in a section titled "Voices from the Darkness."

Not until the concluding four sections, "Solutions," does Doyle allow his indignation to express itself fully. After first slapping the hand of the British government (frequent "remonstrances," he says, while far in excess of what other governments have done, have but "inadequately represented the anger and impatience of those British subjects who were aware of the true state of affairs" [*Crime,* 117]), he turns to a scathing denunciation of the Belgians whose "colony is a scandal before the whole world" (*Crime,* 6).

As for a solution, Doyle angrily contends that, given the behavior of the Belgians, no amount of reform would be acceptable. He proposes that the European powers (Britain, France, and Germany) call a congress to summarily remove the Congo from Belgian jurisdiction and partition it under more benevolent rule. If no such congress can be formed, then he demands that Britain in all good conscience should act alone: "It is our duty, as it has often been in the world's history, to grapple single-handed with that which should be a common task" (*Crime,* 125). Although Doyle feels legally justified when he says that Belgium must be declared "an outlaw state," his ultimate authority is a moral one: "If the Powers join in, or give us a mandate, all the better. But we have a mandate from something higher than the Powers which obliges us to act" (*Crime,* 6).

Although Rudyard Kipling had written to Doyle suggesting that Belgium might "tell us to mind our own affairs (with a few nasty remarks about India thrown in),"[6] any parallels that Belgium might draw to the British East India Company and the British position in India were irrelevant to Doyle. He was not opposed to imperialism or the spread of capitalism; he was opposed to blatant tortures and cruelties in the service of either. In Doyle's view, imperialism was an international extension of the concept of noblesse oblige with a series of rights and responsibilities to be discharged by both the conquered and the conqueror. His indignation was kept for those people who, failing to understand their responsibilities, grossly vi-

olated their part of the bargain. In his view, the white man's burden
was not an onerous one; his contempt was for those who refused to
pick it up.

Doyle the Historian

As a child, Doyle had enthusiastically read the histories of Thomas
Babington Macaulay, so when as an adult he began to write his own
version of the events of his time, it seems natural that he looked
to his favorite historian again. Like that of Macaulay, Doyle's method
of presentation is to state the thesis and the antithesis and then to
show that the balanced judgment, the rational approach, is found
in the synthesis, the amalgamation of both extremes. Like Macaulay,
Doyle also sees history in romantic terms, with the clash of armies
and the ambitions of great men altering the course of the world.
This view of history is so entirely consistent with Doyle's character
that it comes as no surprise that the temptation to see and describe
events in the traditional rosy language of heroism is one that Doyle
cannot resist.

The Great Boer War and "The War in South Africa: Its Cause
and Conduct." Doyle's first foray into the writing of history was,
characteristically, brought about by what he felt was a bitter injustice—in this case, European criticism of British actions in the
Boer War. The form that this criticism was to take had manifested
itself earlier, within his own family, when in October 1899, his
mother had aggressively defended the actions of the Boers by lik-
ening their position to that of a beleaguered David poised to fight
off the Goliath of the British Empire. The Ma'am's staunch espousal
of the cause of the underdog would, in other circumstances, have
been Doyle's own, but in this case he felt that the underdog was
in fact the bigger bully. In a reply to his mother Doyle suggested
that by denying equal rights, and most notably the right to vote,
to people of all nationalities who had worked long and hard for the
South African Republic and deserved the reward of citizenship, the
Boers had shown themselves to be philosophically, if not numeri-
cally, the Goliath. And in further explanation he continued: "As
to the merits of the quarrel: from the day they invaded Natal that
becomes merely academic. But surely it is obvious that they have
prepared for years and that we have not. What becomes of our deep
and sinister designs then?"[7]

Finally, when Paul Kruger, the president of the Republic, led "the stiff-necked" Boers in outright armed rebellion against the British, Doyle felt he had to do more than argue; he had to act. After several unsuccessful attempts to enlist (at forty, he was too old to join the ranks) Doyle was appointed senior civil physician to a private field hospital located at Bloemfontein. During his service in South Africa, he took copious notes on everything that he saw, heard, or had reported to him, but he didn't formalize his analysis until he returned home and saw the full extent of the national and international criticism being leveled at the British government.

Most of this criticism was not as ill-deserved as Doyle perceived it to be. Many of the accusations of widespread looting, brutality, and starvation in the women and children's camps were true, as was the charge that the British had used the soft-nosed "dum-dum" bullets. Doyle, in a nationalistic fervor of indignation, refused to believe in these "stories," as he termed them. Early on, he had made up his mind that the case against the British was a clear injustice, even though, in fact the issue was more complicated and the blame more evenly distributed than Doyle could allow.

At first, he was indignant that there was no official governmental response to the international storm of criticism: "Perhaps we were too proud, perhaps we were too negligent—but the fact was obvious that judgment was being given against us by default." But soon, Doyle, constitutionally incapable of sitting still in the face of injustice, determined on private action: "How *could* they know our case? . . . Why didn't some Briton draw it up? And then like a bullet through my head, came the thought, 'Why don't you draw it up yourself?' " (*MA,* 185).

Doyle wrote "The War in South Africa; Its Cause and Conduct" in two weeks during the close of 1901. In a fury of indignation he wrote to set the record straight, to refute the charges of brutality and neglect of prisoners brought against the British troops, and to defend the national honor. Never before or since, he claims in his autobiography, had he felt such an imperative call to do something.

Because the criticism was so widespread, he wanted the distribution of his pamphlet-book to be equally far-flung. To this end he devised a brilliant marketing plan: If the sixty-thousand-word book was bound cheaply in paper covers, it could be sold for only sixpence, a price which would insure a large domestic market. And if Doyle could establish a fund to underwrite the costs of international publication, including the enormous expense of translation, then his little book would, as he so desperately wanted, reach into every corner of the world.

Doyle's scheme was an instant success; the Intelligence Department at the War Office put all its records at his disposal, the Foreign Office contributed money to his War Book Fund account, Reginald Smith of his publishing company, Smith, Elder and Co., offered to print the book free of charge, and hundreds of private citizens sent donations so that other people could receive the book free of charge. Fifty thousand copies were sold in Britain alone, while twenty thousand copies went to Germany, twenty thousand to France, and substantial numbers to Holland, Russia, Hungary, Sweden, Portugal, Italy, Spain, and Rumania.

Even in his role of defending angel, Doyle is, as always, eager to be fair to both sides, so that the book, which is filled with a sense of honest indignation, is ultimately persuasive because it is so evenhanded. In the introduction to his pamphlet Doyle demonstrates his approach: "There never was a war in history in which the right was absolutely on one side, or in which no incidents of the campaign were open to criticism, I do not pretend that it was so here. But I do not think that any unprejudiced man can read the facts without acknowledging that the British Government has done its best to avoid war, and the British Army to wage it with humanity."[8]

Although both statements are open to question, the tremendous influence of Doyle's personal standing and of his rhetorical style is attested to by the change that did occur in international opinion. By the end of the year, the international press no longer specifically singled out Britain as the chief culprit in the conflict, while on the practical level various grain-producing countries slowed down or ceased their shipments of grain to Kruger. It is clear that no matter what the merits were, Doyle had won a decisive propaganda victory for the British. And as a signal indication of the gratitude felt by his government for all Doyle's help in this particular matter, he was knighted on 9 August 1902 for "outstanding service to the nation."

Some months before Doyle's famous little book appeared in 1900, Smith, Elder and Co. had published his first full-length work of history, *The Great Boer War*. Dedicated to John L. Langman, this book is another testament to Doyle's evenhanded approach as it apparently pleased both the British and the Boers, many of whom wrote unsolicited letters to Doyle complimenting him on his fairness.

Doyle places much of the blame for the war on President Kruger's overweening ambition and arrogance, while his followers, "these children of the veldt," are only guilty of obedience to their chosen leader.[9] As fighters, the Boers are "worthy adversaries," whose tactical skill and bravery cannot be overestimated. Time and time again Doyle pays tribute to the fighting quality of the Boers by drawing attention to their tenacity, ferocity, and adaptability.

Yet, in the final analysis, the bravery of the Boers is not enough because, as he deduces after noting the way in which the Boers abandoned their capital town, they were not "in the better cause" (*Boer War,* 381). And he concludes in a passage reminiscent of *Micah Clarke* that summarizes his position: "From above the Boers came flooding down, dour, resolute, riding silently through the rain, or chanting hymns around their camp-fires—brave honest farmers, but standing unconsciously for mediaevalism and corruption, even as our rough-tongued Tommies stood for civilization, progress and equal rights for all men" (*Boer War,* 185).

Of course, Doyle's language characteristically reflects his heroic view of war. For instance, instead of simply commending the colonial troops, he says that their "excellent behaviour" showed that they were the equals of the regulars "in gallantry." And the accidental death of a lieutenant is given additional drama and pathos in Doyle's rendition: "One leg and the other foot was carried off, as he lay upon the sand bag parapet watching the effect of the British fire. 'There's an end of my cricket,' said the gallant sportsman, and was carried to the rear with a cigar between his clenched teeth" (*Boer War,* 179). Even when Doyle feels that a tactical mistake has been made, that an attack or reconnaissance has little military value, he does not say so directly because he perceives such criticism as a denigration of the sacrifice made by the men, a denigration that Doyle's code will not permit. Of the siege of Mafeking, "an open town which contained no regular soldiers," a town that Doyle was not convinced should ever have been held, never mind besieged, he concludes with: "All this had, at a cost of 200 lives, been done by this one devoted band of men, who killed, wounded, or took not less than one thousand of their opponents. Critics may say that the enthusiasm in the Empire was excessive, but at least it was expended over worthy men and a fine deed of arms" (*Boer War,* 364).

As this book makes evident, it is inconceivable to Doyle that Englishmen can behave in a base or selfish way, especially when the circumstances demand all that is finest of them. Every mistake is therefore described as a "gallant disaster," or "heroic endeavor," while his reproof for a mistake in judgment, if delivered at all, is given in the mildest of terms: "The death of Major Taunton, Captains Knapp and young Brabant . . . was a heavy price to pay for the knowledge that the Boers were in considerable strength to the south" (*Boer War,* 180).

The section of this book that caused the biggest stir was Doyle's concluding chapter titled "Some Military Lessons of the War," in which he contends that many army practices were out of date and must be revamped. In particular, he upset military minds by suggesting that the branch of the army "most in need of reform" was the cavalry, which he said should henceforth be mounted infantry (*Boer War,* 446). "We have never trained any first class infantry yet," he claimed, and went on to say that the Boer War had shown how revolutionary was the concept of mounted marksmen. Some of his suggestions were supported by various members of the armed services (Winston Churchill, for example, was one of Doyle's staunchest supporters), but in the main, the military authorities did not want civilian interference in their affairs. Once the initial storm of protest subsided, though, many of Doyle's reforms were slowly introduced, including the controversial and gradual replacement of cavalry with infantry units.

World War I. After *The Great Boer War* Doyle did not write another history until the start of World War I, an event that he characterized as "the physical climax of my life as it must be of the life of every living man and woman."[10] For some years previous to the outbreak of hostilities, Doyle had refused to take the German threat seriously, for, as he asserted on numerous occasions, he could see no logical reason why Germany should attack Britain.

Doyle's belief in logic as a governing principle in European political affairs was a mistake, but he did not change his mind until 1913 when he read and responded to the open avowal of German aggression contained in a pamphlet written by General Von Bernhardi called "Germany and the Next War." Doyle's response, "Great Britain and the Next War" (1914), painstakingly analyzes and refutes, with historical facts presented in the form of a reasoned defense, Bernhardi's "case" against England. After this careful demolition of all Bernhardi's points, Doyle concludes by admitting that his own former position was a mistake: "Every one of his propositions I dispute. But this is all beside the question. We have not to do with his argument, but with its results. Those results are that he, a man whose opinion is of weight and a member of the ruling class in Germany, tells us frankly that Germany will attack us the moment she sees a favorable opportunity. I repeat that we should be mad if we did not take very serious notice of the warning."[11]

The war that did come about in just the way that Bernhardi had predicted was detailed by Doyle in his most extensive historical work, a six-volume effort titled *A History of the Great War: The British Campaigns.*[12] Published by volume consecutively from 1917 until 1920, *A History of the Great War* attempts to trace the military movements, decisions, engagements, and battles that comprised the five years of the war. In order to simplify this complex undertaking, each volume deals with one year of the war, while the last year, with its intense military activity, is broken down into two volumes, January to July and July to November 1918.

As he had done in the past, Doyle relied heavily on documentation in an effort to give what he saw as a balanced presentation of "the facts." His rhetorical presentation is an indication of his particular view of the writing of history: "It can never be precise but it can be true,"[13] he wrote to his brother at the time, and because he believes that there is a "truth" to be found, and that the writer is capable of an objective stance, he gives his readers "continuous implicit attestations of veracity or appeals to documented historical fact."[14]

After his patriotic success with *The Great Boer War*, Doyle had no trouble obtaining access to all the information he needed for his new work: "Between ourselves I have Smith-Dorrien's diaries and am promised Haig's," he wrote in a letter to his brother Innes, "so on top of Bulfin's I am pretty well informed."[15] In the preface to the first volume Doyle attests to the diverse nature of his sources "whether written (in the form of letters and diaries) or oral (reports from eye-witnesses or military authorities)," but notwithstanding all the information he collected, these volumes clearly reflect one man's view of the war, a man who, while trying to describe and analyze the military conflict that the world was witnessing, was also firmly convinced that the British position was totally correct and, more, that the English-speaking races were generally innately superior to the rest of the participants.

While other, younger authors, notably Siegfried Sassoon, Wilfred Owen, Edmund Blunden, and Robert Graves, came to feel that the war, begun as "a glorious adventure," soon degenerated into an experience so terrible that it was literally "utterly indescribable,"[16] Doyle never felt, or at any rate never expressed, such feelings. As the war progressed, he did come to feel that the conflict was no longer an adventure, but he could not see it as less than glorious. If it was not an adventure, and by 1916 it quite clearly was not, then it had to be something more, not less: a national quest, perhaps? or a spiritual warning of some magnitude? The writer who had espoused, with such enthusiasm, the chivalric code of personal honor in *The White Company* and *Sir Nigel* could not see war, "that feat of arms," as less than ennobling.

Many recent historians have commented on the particular kind of innocence that characterized the British entry into the conflict, and the particular despair and alienation that developed over the course of five years.[17] As a historian, Doyle should be seen as an embodiment of Britain's initial innocence. His remark to his brother on commencing the history clearly illustrates his attitude: "I shall now do a worthy book and it may well be my Magnum Opus for the subject will make it illustrious."[18]

Doyle's language in the work itself reflects this heroic view. As in his writing on the Boer War, he continues to employ sporting metaphors (troops "wrestle" for positions, or advance by "carrying the ball forward") and uplifting language in an effort to assign dignity to the men and splendor to their cause. Troops are "battle-weary but still indomitable" (6:113), a battalion cut off from its lines without reinforcements is "sustained by some prophetic vision of an imminent victory" (6:134), and a heavy bombardment is made light of as "the attrition was going merrily forward" (6:113). When he does have to record a retreat or a blunder, he does so in terms that, while allowing for a sense of disappointment, manage to suggest the possibility of glory even in the heart of failure. After one of the less successful British attacks, at the Battle of Loos at the end of 1915, he says: "On the whole, it must be admitted that, although ground was gained . . . the losses were so heavy and the results so barren that there was no adequate return for the splendid efforts of the men" (2:235–36).

In keeping with this rhetorical position, his descriptions of the Germans as a race, as opposed to the examples of individual German bravery and kindness that he never fails to praise, show them to be unregenerate villains. In chapter 1, volume 1, "The Breaking of

Peace," he says of the representations being made by the German ambassador that, "these assurances were continued almost to the moment of the arrival of German troops in Belgium, and give me one more instance of the absolute want of truth and honour which from the days of Frederick the Great has been the outstanding characteristic of German diplomacy" (1:19). In volume 2, chapter 1, the German soldiers who are responsible for introducing that "diabolical agency," poison gas, are described as having "sold their souls as soldiers but the Devil's price was a poor one" (2:50). And, from this point on, the Germans are most often referred to as the "Teutonic barbarians" or the "pestilential hordes."

In contrast to the barbarians, the leader of the Allies, by the end of 1915, Douglas Haig, is described in terms befitting his role as savior: "He was a man of the type which the British love who shines the brighter against a dark background. Youthful for so high a command, and with a frame and spirit which were even younger than his years, with the caution of a Scotchman and the calculated dash of a leader of cavalry, he was indeed the ideal man for a great military crisis" (2:247). While many historians, feeling that Sir Douglas Haig was incompetent at best, would take exception to Doyle's estimate of Haig,[19] the description does demonstrate Doyle's rather simplistic view of the conflict as one in which the forces of evil are ranged against the forces of good.

Much of volume 1 is given up to a summary of the political events that led to the war, but the first battle of Mons provides the reader with a good example of Doyle's work as a military historian. This action, which was spread over the three days of 23 to 26 August, is precisely reported down to the smallest detail. Doyle shows the disposition of all the troops involved, noting the placement of individual divisions and even of individual guns within each division. Each movement, attack, or feint attack is carefully traced. Beginning with the moment of the initial artillery encounter and ending with the German commander's "exultant telegram" of success to Berlin when the British forces retreated, Doyle leaves none of the military details unreported.

Although he makes no attempt to justify in military terms the huge numbers of dead and wounded left behind by the carnage that was World War I, he does offer the reader his attempt to make sense of the war. Such a large sacrifice must, he explains, be justified within some larger scheme, even if that scheme is not yet clear to us: "With the deep conviction that the final results of this great convulsion are meant to be spiritual rather than material and that upon an enlightened recognition of this depends the future history of mankind" (6:305).

This view is further elaborated when, after claiming, ironically as it turned out, that World War I was "the greatest war that ever has been, or in all probability ever will be," Doyle suggests that such a catastrophe must be seen as the catalyst for change: "Personal and national selfishness" must be put aside in order for the world to find that path that leads to "the City Beautiful upon the distant hills" (6:306). Doyle argues that, like the poison gas in *The Poison Belt,* the war must be viewed as a terrible warning to mankind. The purpose, he concludes, was "not to change rival frontiers, but to mould the hearts and spirits of men—there lies the explanation and justification of all that we have endured" (6:305).

The Spiritualist

Doyle's decision to publicly endorse Spiritualism, a decision that was to cost him a great deal both in terms of his personal popularity and of his own personal fortune, was made as part of his assessment of the meaning of World War I. He believed that the only way to respond to such a catastrophic warning was for people to learn to be more humane, more generous, and more loving, and less materialistic and selfish. The world could not go on unchanged. His experience of the war years, including the loss of his son, brother, and brother-in-law, was the catalyst that prompted him to action, but his decision to embrace Spiritualism was far from a quick response to a series of unconscionable events. Doyle, who had previously termed himself a skeptical observer, had been interested in Spiritualism since 1887, when he detailed a séance he had attended. As his writings demonstrate, he had been plagued during the intervening years by a growing sense of personal disillusionment and weariness. This feeling, in combination with the warning provided by the war, was the catalyst for Doyle.

Many of his admirers were and are bewildered and angered by his turn to the spiritual world, but Doyle's embracing of Spiritualism is surely a logical outcome for a man who had rejected all institutionalized religions, yet never stopped searching for something to ascribe meaning to the jumble of human experience. Spiritualism, a philosophy which eschewed the divisiveness of other religions, offered Doyle a philosophy of hope without any of the constraints of dogmatism, a combination that, given his personality, was understandably attractive. That the belief he found was predicated on the notion of building a bridge between this world and the world hereafter added precisely that touch of mystery and adventure that Doyle found irresistible. Also, by providing a completed world, filled with people, a social hierarchy, customs, and manners that emphasized loving-kindness and personal responsibility, the Spiritualists enabled Doyle to transmute the pessimism of his life into an eternal optimism.

Given Doyle's personality, it was to be expected that, once having been convinced by Spiritualism, he could do no less than devote his life to its advocacy. The cause was too much the underdog for Doyle not to defend it vigorously and, just as earlier in his life he refused to modify his anti-Catholicism to please his family, so now he would refuse to compromise his belief in Spiritualism to please his public.

A declaration of faith.   The date of Doyle's first book on this subject, *The New Revelation,* was 1918, the same year that the Great War ended, yet significantly, he dedicated this work to a group of soldiers fighting another battle: "To all the brave men and women, humble or learned, who have had the moral courage during seventy years to face ridicule or worldly disadvantage in order to testify to an all-important truth."[20]

Doyle's purpose in writing *The New Revelation* was twofold. First, he wanted to detail the steps of his progression from skeptical observer to fervent believer; second, he wanted to warn the world, in a more direct way than he felt had been possible earlier, of the spiritual danger that surrounded them. Doyle quotes "a celebrated Psychic, Mrs. Piper" who had prophesied in 1899 that "a terrible war in different parts of the world" would end, leaving the world "purified and cleansed" and ready for a state of perfection, but he uses *The New Revelation* to emphasize that only the first half of Mrs. Piper's prophecy has come true; "the second half remains to be fulfilled," he warns in the preface (*Revelation,* viii).

This 120-page book, and, in fact, all of Doyle's writings henceforth, the rest of his life, his prestige, and his fortune, were dedicated to making the world aware that the second half of this prophecy must be made to come true: "I seemed suddenly to see that this subject with which I had so long dallied was not merely a study of a force outside the rules of science, but that it was really something tremendous, a breaking down of the walls between two worlds, a direct undeniable message from beyond, a call of hope and guidance to the human race at the time of its deepest affliction" (*Revelation,* 39).

The following year (1919) Doyle wrote and published *The Vital Message.* Taken together, these two small volumes comprise a cogent introduction to Doyle's view of Spiritualism, including his own version of what the spirit world looked like—"Happy circles live in pleasant homesteads with every amenity of beauty and of music"[21]—along with an examination of the doctrines underlying Spiritualist belief and his thoughts about Christianity in relation to the modern world. The last subject is given particular emphasis in *The Vital Message,* a volume that, as its title suggests, has an urgent thesis to proclaim: that Christianity has failed in its purpose, "the churches are empty husks, which contained no spiritual food for the human race" (*VM,* 15).

Doyle goes on to argue that the Spiritualists revere Christ's life for its "consistent record of charity, breadth of mind, unselfishness, courage, reason and progressiveness" (*VM,* 15). Thus, Doyle links Spiritualism and Christian principles so that the conclusion, in which he suggests that Spiritualism is the system of belief tailored to replace an outworn Christianity, is a logical outcome of his former thesis. "This new wave of inspiration which has been sent in to the world by God" is, he says, the only religion now capable of turning the world away from "active materialism" and back to "the very teaching of that Master" so long ignored (*VM,* 139). Although these two books are clearly instructive in relation to Doyle's thoughts and beliefs, they are also instructive about the nature of Spiritualism (or as its adherents preferred to call it, psychical research).

The Society for Psychical Research had had a number of famous presidents, including William Crookes, William James, and A.J. Balfour, as well as many distinguished members, including Edmund Guney, Malcolm Gutherie, Sir Oliver Lodge (who was, coincidentally, knighted on the same day as Doyle), and Frederic Myers. Far from being a single erring mystic, Doyle found himself, by the end of the nineteenth century, in very good company in a well-established movement. Most of these men were interested in proving scientifically that the claims made by the Spiritualists were true, and, initially, Doyle also had been concerned with determining the scientific basis of Spiritualism. In an effort to be objective, he records in *The New Revelation,* (28) his disappointments and anger at the failure of many of his early efforts: "I could see no such proof, and they left me simply bewildered."

But, once he had fully accepted what he termed "the science of religion," he turned more and more to the moral and religious side of his new belief, becoming less and less interested in scientific proofs or experiments no matter what their results. Doyle had long espoused scientific rationalism: in fact, as a young man he had attacked Catholicism precisely because it demanded an act of faith not susceptible to proof. However, as an advocate of Spiritualism he demonstrated the same kind of single-minded belief that had characterized his Catholic relatives. To all scientific claims about fraudulent mediums, dishonest séances, and so on, Doyle simply retorted that as there are dishonest people, so of course there must be dishonest Spiritualists. Against all charges of fraud, he offered only his own knowledge, his own sincerity, as a refutation of what he would once have tried to disprove.

Fairies and Journeys

Once he had completely accepted Spiritualism, Doyle was open to many charges of gullibility and naïveté. In one famous case, the photographs of the Cottingley fairies, Doyle's credulity was exposed and as a consequence his reputation diminished. The incident, described in his book, *The Coming of the Fairies,* as "either the most elaborate and ingenious hoax," or "an event in human history which is epoch-making,"[22] concerns some photographs of fairies taken in 1920 by a young girl, Elsie Wright, and her cousin Frances, who "are said to have played with fairies and elves in the woods near the village since babyhood" (*Fairies,* 16).

There was no question that the photographs existed; the question was, were they contrived? There was a great deal of evidence given by the Kodak Co. and other professional users of film as to the possibilities of superimposition and other forms of trick photography. Doyle, however, remained "quite convinced of their entire genuineness," not on the basis of any scientific evidence, but because of the "evidence of transparent honesty and simplicity" of the people involved (*Fairies,* 36).

As part of Doyle's belief that he was one of the few entrusted with the duty to educate by preaching and writing, he undertook a two-volume work on *The History of Spiritualism*.[23] The first volume, published in 1924, deals with some of the accumulated evidence, which he discusses and analyzes, of the first hundred years of Spiritualism. The second volume, published in 1926, brings the reader up to date with all the contemporary developments, many of them witnessed and attested to by the writer, and concludes with a reiteration of one of Doyle's firmest beliefs—that the cruel meaninglessness of life can be, first, mitigated by explanation, and, second, vanquished by a belief in the idealism postulated in the Spiritualist doctrines.

Throughout all his writing and preachings, Doyle emphasizes two central points: the failure of organized religion to stop what he called "the mounting tide of materialism"[24] and the emergence of a positive religion or idealism that had proven, Doyle believed, that it had the means to turn the world in a different direction. He was fifty-eight when he embraced Spiritualism, yet he threw himself into this new phase of his life with the same kind of single-minded energy that characterized everything he had ever done. As a measure of the strength of a faith that was to sustain and comfort him for the last thirteen years of his life, he ends his autobiography (written in 1923) with a declaration: "That is the work [Spiritualism] which will occupy, either by voice or pen, the remainder of my life. What immediate shape it will take I cannot say. Human plans are vain things, and it is better for the tool to lie passive until the great hand moves it once more" (*MA*, 399).

Chapter Eight
Conclusion

Arthur Conan Doyle is one of the few remaining major Victorian writers who has not been "rediscovered" by contemporary critics. Perhaps this is because, as the author of the Sherlock Holmes stories, Doyle is only remembered by the modern reader as the creator of that most famous detective. The Holmes fictions are read as widely now as they were when they first appeared, and the recent rash of stories that use the minutiae of Holmes's life as their starting point attest further to the longevity of the Holmes magic. Unfortunately, the Holmes magic is so powerful that it has worked a kind of disappearing act on his creator and on the rest of his creator's work. A striking example of the neglectful treatment accorded Doyle is the vast number of books devoted to Sherlockian matters—a biography of Holmes, a study of Holmes's writings, and a historical analysis of the various timetables used by Holmes, for example—which far exceed the works devoted to his creator.

Of the scholarly works concerned with Sherlock Holmes, the best associate the detective character and the form of the detective story with the romance. Dorothy Sayers, for example, claims that the detective is "the latest of the popular heroes, the true successor of Roland and Lancelot,"[1] while G. K. Chesterton credits Doyle "under the fantastic form of the minutiae of Sherlock Holmes"[2] with turning London into the elfland inhabited by the fairy prince in older narratives. Nor did this association go unnoticed in Doyle's time. Speaking of detectives in 1893, a journalist complained, "There has been of late a noticeable tendency to glorify the detective's trade and invest it with an air of romance."[3] Doyle did just that, creating a character and a world that captured so precisely an imaginative golden place and time that, as Vincent Starrett says, "Here, though the world explode, these two survive. . . . And it is always eighteen ninety-five."[4]

The knight-errant turned detective, and the moral view of the world that he embodies, are fundamental to all Doyle's work. Doyle's portrayal of a heroic code, demonstrated through the actions of his

archetypal protagonists, including the great detective, is an attempt
to be ethically corrective, to set a standard to aim for, in the face
of human weaknesses and foibles. As a man Doyle attempted to live
his own life in the same way, demonstrating in all his undertakings
an enduring concern for fair play and justice, a belief in the concept
of honor, and a commitment to a chivalric code of behavior. In any
estimation of his achievements, therefore, it is important to look
at his work as a whole to see the consistency with which he maintained his moral position and the part that his various works play
in its exposition.

Undoubtedly Doyle, "the diversified genius," will receive his "full
accounting"[5] as the writers of the late Victorian period continue to
be closely scrutinized by critics. The general reader meanwhile can
turn or return with pleasure to the writer who produced *The White
Company, The Lost World, Rodney Stone,* and *Sir Nigel,* as well as all
the excellent short stories, for Doyle is an eminently satisfying writer
of adventure and romance who deserves to be read. In the final
analysis, the complexity and stature of this writer can be seen by
readers who apply Doyle's standard for narrative to his own work.
Fiction, Doyle said, is supposed to provide dreams, to present "that
one window of imagination which leads out into the enchanted
country."[6] As a purveyor of that "window of imagination" Doyle
is an extremely interesting and complex Victorian writer.

Notes and References

Preface

1. *Memories and Adventures* (Boston: Little Brown & Co., 1924), 68; hereafter cited in the text as *MA*.
2. Adrian Conan Doyle, *The True Conan Doyle* (New York: Coward-McCann, 1946), 3.
3. Ibid, 30.

Chapter One

1. Quoted in Doyle, *The True Conan Doyle*, 11.
2. Quoted in Charles Higham, *The Adventures of Conan Doyle: The Life of the Creator of Sherlock Holmes* (New York: W. W. Norton & Co., 1976), 31.
3. *The Stark Munro Letters*, (London: Longmans Green & Co., 1895), 19–20; hereafter cited in the text as *SM*.
4. See Higham, *Adventures*, 114.
5. Quoted in John Dickson Carr, *The Life of Sir Arthur Conan Doyle* (New York: Harper, 1949), 144.
6. Ibid., 159.
7. Ibid.
8. Quoted in Doyle, *The True Conan Doyle*, 7.
9. Ibid., 30.

Chapter Two

1. George Saintsbury, *A History of Nineteenth Century Literature* (London, 1896), 338.
2. Ibid., 337.
3. Robert Kiely, *Robert Louis Stevenson and the Fiction of Adventure* (Cambridge, Mass.: Harvard University Press, 1964), 21.
4. Ibid., 3. A collection of Zola's essays, not available in England until 1893, was published in France in 1880, where they were read by R. L. Stevenson.
5. See Robert Louis Stevenson's essays "A Gossip on Romance" and "A Note on Realism" in *Memories and Portraits*, (New York: C. Scribner's Sons, 1895).
6. Kiely, *Robert Louis Stevenson*, 7.
7. Ibid., 20.

8. Quoted in Kennneth Graham, *English Criticism of the Novel 1865–1900* (Oxford: Oxford University Press, 1965), 66.

9. Northrop Frye, *Anatomy of Criticism* (Princeton, N.J.: Princeton University Press, 1957), 187.

10. "The Mystery of the Sasassa Valley," in *The Gully of Bluemansdyke and Other Stories* (Freeport, N.Y.: Books for Libraries Press, 1970), 236.

11. Carr, *Life,* 61.

12. Ibid.

13. Higham, *Adventures,* 57.

14. John Cawelti, *Adventure, Mystery, and Romance* (Chicago: Chicago University Press, 1981), 43.

15. Ibid., 48.

16. Higham, *Adventures,* 58.

17. "The Captain of the Pole-Star," in *The Captain of the Polestar and Other Tales* (Freeport, N.Y.: Books for Libraries Press, 1970); hereafter cited in the text as *Polestar.*

18. Higham, *Adventures,* 61.

19. Kiely, *Robert Louis Stevenson,* 198.

20. Ibid.

21. Dick Allen and David Chacko, eds., *Detective Fiction: Crime and Compromise* (New York: Harcourt, Brace & Jovanovich, 1974), vii.

22. Dorothy Sayers, quoted in Allen and Chacko, *Detective Fiction,* vii.

Chapter Three

1. Quoted in A. E. Murch, *The Development of the Detective Novel* (New York: Philosophical Library, 1958), 71.

2. Ibid., 80.

3. Ibid., 124.

4. Ibid., 68.

5. Colin Ousby, *Bloodhounds of Heaven* (Cambridge, Mass.: Harvard University Press, 1976), 136.

6. Charles Higham is one of Doyle's biographers who takes exception to this view of the reception given to *A Study in Scarlet.* In his book *The Adventures of Conan Doyle,* Higham argues that the favorable reviews reprinted on the flyleaf of the book testify to the novel's critical success. However, while the reviews are encouraging, two are from small provincial newspapers and only one (excerpted from the *Scotsman*) carried any literary weight.

7. *A Study in Scarlet* in *The Complete Sherlock Holmes,* 2 vols. (Garden City, N.Y.: Doubleday & Co., 1927) 1:15; hereafter cited in the text as *CH.* This editon is the most reliable and currently available.

8. See Murch, *Development of the Detective Novel,* 100.

9. Joseph Campbell, *The Hero with a Thousand Faces* (New York: Signet Classics, 1956), 28.
10. See Carr, *Life,* 88.
11. See Campbell, *The Hero,* 28.
12. See Ousby, *Bloodhounds of Heaven,* 141.
13. Quoted in Carr, *Life,* 98.
14. Ibid., 100.
15. Ibid.

Chapter Four

1. For a full discussion of this issue, see Helen Cam's essay, "The Historical Novel" in Routledge & Kegan Paul pamphlet (historical association pamphlet number G.48), Great Britain, 1961.
2. Frye, *Anatomy of Criticism,* 187.
3. Thomas Babington Macauley, *History of England,* vols. 1 and 2 appeared in 1848, vols. 3 and 4 in 1855; vol. 5 was published posthumously in 1861.
4. Quoted in Pierre Nordon, *Conan Doyle,* trans. Frances Partridge. (New York: Holt, Rinehart & Winston, 1967), 288.
5. *Micah Clarke* (New York: Harper & Brothers, 1889). All further page references will be to this edition and cited hereafter in the text as *MC.*
6. See Frye, *Anatomy of Criticism,* 186.
7. See Campbell, *The Hero,* 210.
8. For a fuller treatment of this argument, see Nordon, *Conan Doyle,* 286–97.
9. Quoted in Carr, *Life,* 83.
10. Andrew Lang, *Adventures among Books* (London: Longmans, Green & Co., 1905), 279–80.
11. *The White Company* (London: Smith, Elder & Co., 1891), 6; hereafter cited in the text as *WC.*
12. Nordon, *Conan Doyle,* 309.
13. See Carr, *Life,* 86.
14. Ibid.
15. Ibid.
16. Ibid.
17. Amy Cruse, *The Victorians and Their Reading,* (London: Houghton Mifflin Co., 1935), 34.
18. Quoted in Carr, *Life,* 102.
19. Ibid., 135.
20. Ibid., 147.
21. Ibid., 148.

22. *Uncle Bernac* (New York: D. Appleton & Co., 1897), 158; hereafter cited in the text as *Bernac.*

23. See Nordon, *Conan Doyle,* 312.

24. *Sir Nigel* (New York: McClure, Phillips & Co., 1906), 116; hereafter cited in the text as *Nigel.*

25. See Nordon, *Conan Doyle,* 312.

26. Ibid., 313.

Chapter Five

1. Cawelti, *Adventure, Mystery, Romance,* 104.

2. Carr, *Life,* 243.

3. Ibid., 224.

4. Ibid., 246.

5. Ibid.

6. Ibid., 219.

7. Ibid., 217.

8. Ibid.

9. Jacques Barzun, quoted in *Detective Fiction: Twentieth Century Views,* ed. Robin W. Winks (Englewood Cliffs, N.J.: Prentice-Hall, 1980), 152.

10. Robert Louis Stevenson, *The Dynamiter* (London: Longmans Green, 1922), 26–28.

11. For a longer discussion of the semiotic aspects of Holmes, see Thomas A. Sebeok and Jean Umiker-Sebeok, "You Know My Method: A Juxtaposition of Charles S. Pierce and Sherlock Holmes," *Semiotica* 26, nos. 3–4 (1979).

12. See Carr, *Life,* 348.

13. Ibid., 349.

14. Carl Burton, "The Development of the Detective Hero," Ph.D. diss., Columbia University, 1974, 285.

15. Ibid., 287.

16. For a full evaluation and description of these stories—largely undervalued by critics—see Higham, *Adventures.*

17. See Ousby, *Bloodhounds of Heaven,* 172.

18. Ibid., 173.

Chapter Six

1. Quoted in Peter Costello, *Jules Verne: Inventor of Science Fiction* (London: Hodder & Stoughton, 1978), 74.

2. Quoted in I. O. Evans, *Jules Verne and His Work* (Boston: Twayne, 1966), 156.

3. "Danger," in *The Best Science Fiction of Arthur Conan Doyle,* Charles G. Waugh and Martin H. Greenberg eds. (Carbondale, Ill.: Southern

Illinois University Press, 1981), 140; further references to this volume are cited in the text as *BSF*.

4. Quoted in Carr, *Life*, 85.

5. *The Lost World* (New York: Review of Reviews Company, 1912); hereafter cited in the text as *LW*.

6. Quoted in Carr, *Life*, 319.

7. Waugh and Greenberg, introduction to *Best Science Fiction*, ix.

8. Nordon, *Conan Doyle*, 330.

9. James L. Campbell, Sr., "Arthur Conan Doyle," in *Science Fiction Writers*, ed. E. F. Bleiler (New York: Scribner's, 1982).

10. See Carr, *Life*, 320.

11. This same zoologist was a friend to H. G. Wells. He assisted in the writing of the first volume of Wells's *Outline of History*, a volume that begins with a fearsome illustration of two pterodactyls looking just as Doyle described them.

12. See Carr, *Life*, 320.

13. *The Poison Belt* (London: W. H. Allen & Co., 1985), 21; hereafter cited in the text as *PB*.

14. See Nordon, *Conan Doyle*, 329.

15. *The Land of Mist* (Garden City, N.Y.: George H. Doran Co., 1926), 13; hereafter cited in the text as *LM*.

16. Mustard gas, machine guns, and barbed wire were all wartime inventions that epitomized what Doyle, I. A. Richards, Robert Graves, and others felt to be the dehumanized nature of science.

17. Campbell, "Arthur Conan Doyle," 48.

18. Quoted in Carr, *Life*, 411.

19. Waugh and Greenberg, introduction to *Best Science Fiction*, xix.

20. Ibid., xv.

Chapter Seven

1. Carr, *Life*, 310.

2. Ibid.

3. Ibid., 221.

4. Nordon, *Conan Doyle*, 136.

5. *The Crime of the Congo* (London: Hutchinson & Co., 1909), 1; hereafter cited in the text as *Crime*.

6. Ronald Pearsall, *Conan Doyle: A Biographical Solution* (New York: St. Martin's Press, 1977), 121.

7. Quoted in Carr, *Life*, 186.

8. Ibid., 231.

9. *The Great Boer War* (New York: McClure, Phillips & Co., 1900), 372; hereafter cited in the text as *Boer War*.

10. Pearsall, *Conan Doyle*, 141.

11. *Great Britain and the Next War* (Boston: Small, Maynard & Co., 1914), 48.

12. *A History of the Great War* (New York: George H. Doran Co., 1915–20) (American edition of *The British Campaign in France and Flanders*); hereafter cited in the text with references to volume and page.

13. See Nordon, *Conan Doyle*, 92.

14. Paul Fussell, *The Great War and Modern Memory* (London: Oxford University Press, 1974), 310.

15. See Nordon, *Conan Doyle*, 92.

16. See Fussell, *The Great War*, 170.

17. See Barbara Tuchman, *The Guns of August* (New York: Macmillan & Co., 1962) for a description of the innocence with which the British entered this war.

18. See Nordon, *Conan Doyle*, 92.

19. See Paul Fussell, *The Great War*, for a stinging denunciation of Haig as a leader, and Bernard Bergonzi's *Hero's Twilight: A Study of the Literature of the Great War* (London: Constable, 1980) for a further elaboration of this theme.

20. *The New Revelation* (New York: George H. Doran Co., 1918), dedication; hereafter cited in the text as *Revelation*.

21. *The Vital Message* (New York: George H. Doran Co., 1919), 95; hereafter cited in the text as *VM*.

22. *The Coming of the Fairies* (London: Hodder & Stoughton, 1922), 2, 16; hereafter cited in the text as *Fairies*.

23. *The History of Spiritualism*, 2 vols. (New York: George H. Doran Co., 1926).

24. Nordon, *Conan Doyle*, 159.

Chapter Eight

1. Dorothy Sayers, "The Omnibus of Crime," reprinted in Allen and Chacko, *Detective Fiction*, 355.

2. G. K. Chesterton, "A Defense of Detective Stories," in Allen and Chacko, *Detective Fiction*, 385.

3. "*Espionage* as a Profession," *Spectator*, 18 February 1893, 221–22.

4. Vincent Starrett, ed., "221B," quoted by Philip Shreffler in *The Baker Street Reader* (Westport, Conn.: Greenwood Press, 1984).

5. Alvin E. Rodin and Jack D. Kay, eds., *Medical Casebook of Arthur Conan Doyle* (Melbourne, Fla.: Krieger Publishing Co., 1984), preface.

6. Quoted in Nordon, *Conan Doyle*, 339.

Selected Bibliography

PRIMARY SOURCES

1. The Non-Holmes Novels
(Periodical publication dates are given in parentheses.)
Micah Clarke. New York: Harper & Brothers, 1889.
The Firm of Girdlestone; A Romance of the Unromantic. London: Chatto & Windus, 1890.
The White Company. London: Smith, Elder & Co., 1891. (*Cornhill Magazine,* January–December 1891; *New York Sun,* May–August 1891.)
The Doings of Raffles Haw. London: Cassell & Co., 1892. Reprinted, 1912.
The Fate of Fenella. New York: Cassell & Co., 1892. No English edition. (Twenty-four chapters, each by different authors who were familiar with the preceding chapters. Doyle wrote chapter 4.)
The Great Shadow. Bristol, England: Arrowsmith, 1893. (*Louisville Courier–Journal,* 2 October–6 November 1892; *Chicago Tribune,* same dates.)
The Refugees. London: Longmans, Green & Co., 1893. (*Harper's* magazine, January–December 1893.)
The Parasite. London: Constable & Co., 1894. (*Harper's* weekly, November–December 1984.)
The Stark Munro Letters. London: Longmans, Green & Co., 1895. (*Idler,* October 1894–November 1895; *Leslie's Weekly,* December 1894–April 1895.)
Rodney Stone. London: Smith, Elder & Co., 1896. (*Strand,* January–December 1896.)
Uncle Bernac. New York: D. Appleton & Co., 1897. (*Queen,* January–March 1897; *Cosmopolitan Magazine,* same dates.)
The Tragedy of the Korosko. London: Smith, Elder & Co., 1898. (*Strand,* May–December 1897; *American Strand,* June 1897–January 1898.)
A Duet, With an Occasional Chorus. London: Grant Richards, 1899.
Sir Nigel. London: Smith, Elder & Co., 1906. (*Strand,* December 1905–December 1906.)
The Lost World. London: Hodder & Stoughton, 1912. (*Strand,* April–November 1912.) The more readily available edition is Pocket Classics (Gloucester, England: Alan Sutton, 1984).
The Poison Belt. London: Hodder & Stoughton, 1913. (*Strand,* March–July 1913.) The more readily available edition is *The Adventures of Professor Challenger* (London: W. H. Allen & Co., 1985) which con-

tains all the Challenger stories except *The Lost World*. *The Professor Challenger Stories* (London: John Murray, 1952) has the complete collection.

The Land of Mist. London: Hutchinson & Co., 1926. (*Strand*, July 1925– March 1926.)

2. The Non-Holmes Collected Stories

(This lists those collections published in Doyle's lifetime. The note following indicates which editions are still available and those which have been recently reprinted.)

Dreamland and Ghostland. London: Redway, n.d. (ca. 1889).

The Captain of the "Pole Star" and Other Tales. London: Longmans, Green & Co., 1890. (This edition is still available.)

The Gully of Bluemansdyke. London: Walter Scott, 1893. (This edition is currently available.)

My Friend the Murderer. New York: Lovell, Coneyell & Co., 1893.

Round the Red Lamp and Other Tales of Medical Life. London: Methuen & Co., 1894.

The Great Keinplatz Experiment. Chicago: Rand McNally & Co., 1894. (This edition is currently available.)

The Exploits of the Brigadier. London: George Newnes, 1896. (A new Pocket Classics edition of these stories was published in 1984.)

The Man From Archangel and Other Tales. New York: Street & Smith, 1898. (This edition is still available.)

The Green Flag. London: Smith, Elder & Co., 1900.

Stories of War and Sport. New York: D. Appleton & Co., 1902.

The Adventures of Gerard. London: George Newnes, 1903.

Round the Fire Stories. London: Smith, Elder & Co., 1908.

The Last Galley. London: Smith, Elder & Co., 1908. (This edition is still available.)

Danger! and Other Stories. London: John Murray, 1919. (This edition is still available.)

3. Omnibus Editions

Conan Doyle's Best Books. New York: Collier & Son, n.d. (ca. 1911).

The Conan Doyle Stories. London: John Murray, 1922. Six volumes, including 1. *Tales of the Ring & Camp;* 2. *Tales of Pirates & Blue Water;* 3. *Tales of Terror & Mystery;* 4. *Tales of Twilight & the Unseen;* 5. *Tales of Adventure and Medical Life;* and 6. *Tales of Long Ago*.

The Works of Conan Doyle. New York: W.J. Black, 1928.

The Maracot Deep and Other Stories. London: John Murray, 1929.

The Conan Doyle Historical Romances. London: John Murray, 1930. Two volumes, long and short stories: *The White Company, Sir Nigel, Micah*

Clarke, The Refugees, Rodney Stone, Uncle Bernac, and the Brigadier
Gerard stories.

Uncollected Stories: The Unknown Conan Doyle. Edited by John M. Gibson
and Richard L. Green. New York: Doubleday & Co., 1982. Draws
together thirty-three diverse stories from Doyle's work that serve as
a good introduction to the author's narrative skills.

4. The Holmes Novels and Stories

A Study in Scarlet. London: Ward Lock & Co., 1888. (First appeared in
its entirety in *Beeton's Christmas Annual* for 1887.)

The Sign of Four. London: Spencer Blackett, 1890. (*Lippincott's Magazine,*
February 1890.)

The Adventures of Sherlock Holmes. London: George Newnes, 1892. (The
first twelve stories, originally published in the *Strand,* July 1891–
December 1892.)

The Memoirs of Sherlock Holmes. London: George Newnes, 1894. (The second
series of twelve stories, published in the *Strand,* December 1892–
November 1893, as additional episodes of *The Adventures.*)

The Hound of the Baskervilles. London: George Newnes, 1902. (*Strand,*
August 1901–April 1902.)

The Return of Sherlock Holmes. London: George Newnes, 1905. Thirteen
stories. (*Strand,* 1903 and January 1905.)

The Valley of Fear. London: Smith, Elder & Co., 1915. (*Strand,* September
1914–May 1915.)

His Last Bow. London: John Murray, 1917. Seven stories. (*Strand,* September 1908–September 1917.

The Case Book of Sherlock Holmes. London: John Murray, 1927. The final
twelve stories. (*Strand,* October 1921–April 1927).

COLLECTIONS AND OMNIBUS EDITIONS

Sherlock Holmes: The Complete Short Stories. London: John Murray, 1929.

Sherlock Holmes: The Complete Long Stories. London: John Murray, 1929.

The Complete Sherlock Holmes. Garden City, N.Y.: Doubleday & Co., 1930.
The definitive two-volume omnibus, with the famous introduction
by Christopher Morley, "In Memoriam Sherlock Holmes."

A Treasury of Sherlock Holmes. Edited by Adrian Conan Doyle. Garden City,
N.Y.: Hanover House, 1955. Twenty-seven of the short stories plus
A Study in Scarlet and *The Hound of the Baskervilles.* Introduction by
the editor.

The Annotated Sherlock Holmes. New York: Clarkson N. Potter, 1967. 2
vols. The definitive annotated edition, edited by William Baring-
Gould.

The Original Illustrated Sherlock Holmes. Secaucus, N.J.: Castle Books, 1981.
Includes the first three volumes of the short stories plus *The Hound*

of the Baskervilles reproduced in facsimile as they first appeared in the *Strand*.

In 1974, J. Murray, London, issued a reprint of the first editions of the collected stories and the novels. In addition the same material is also available in the series of paperback volumes published, by arrangement with the estate of Sir Arthur Conan Doyle, by Berkley Mystery Books.

5. Histories

The Great Boer War. New York: McClure, Phillips & Co., 1900.

The German War. London and New York: Hodder & Stoughton, 1914.

A History of the Great War: The British Campaigns. 6 volumes. New York: George H. Doran Co., 1915–1920. (The American edition of *The British Campaign in France and Flanders*.)

6. Spiritualist Writings

The New Revelation. New York: George H. Doran Co., 1918.

The Vital Message. New York: George H. Doran Co., 1919.

Spiritualism & Rationalism. New York: George H. Doran Co., 1920.

The Wanderings of a Spiritualist. New York: George H. Doran Co., 1921.

The Coming of the Fairies. London: Hodder & Stoughton, Ltd., 1922.

The Case for Spirit Photography. London: Hutchinson, 1922.

The History of Spiritualism. 2 volumes. New York: George H. Doran Co., 1926.

7. Pamphlets on Public Issues

The War in South Africa, Its Cause and Conduct. London: Smith, Elder, 1902.

The Crime of the Congo. London: Hutchinson & Co., 1909.

The Case for Oscar Slater. London: Hodder & Stoughton, 1912.

Great Britain and the Next War. Boston: Small, Maynard & Company, 1914.

8. Poems

The Guards Came Through and Other Poems. London: J. Murray, 1910.

Songs of the Road. London: Smith, Elder, 1911.

Songs of Action. London: Smith, Elder, 1916.

9. Plays

The Story of Waterloo. London: Samuel French, 1900.

The Speckled Band: An Adventure of Sherlock Holmes. London and New York: Samuel French, 1912.

Sherlock Holmes, A Drama in Four Acts. (with William Gillette) Garden City, N.Y.: Doubleday, Doran & Co., 1935.

10. Autobiography

Memories and Adventures. Boston: Little Brown & Co., 1924. Even though Doyle is silent on those personal matters where the reader most wishes him to be fulsome, this informative account is the best place to begin to understand the author.

SECONDARY SOURCES

The books and articles that follow are necessarily selective, not because there is a large body of critical work on Doyle's writings—there is not—but because of the extraordinary number of publications devoted to writings *about* Holmes. There is a growing body of serious scholarly work on detective fiction and Holmes as a fictional construct—which I have indicated—but critical studies on the rest of Doyle's work are scandalously few and far between. Fulfilling Doyle's worst fears of the appeal of his character, Holmes has, it appears, continued to overshadow the bulk of his creator's work. In an effort to redress the balance, I have included those books and articles that best suggest the direction that serious critics might take; I have only included a few examples of the Holmesian (in Britain) or Sherlockian (in the United States) writings. For those readers who are interested in pursuing this latter approach, *The Baker Street Journal: An Irregular Quarterly of Sherlockiana,* published in New York, or the semiannual *Sherlock Holmes Journal,* published in London, provide the best introduction.

1. Bibliographic Guides
Green, R.L., ed. *A Bibliography of A. Conan Doyle.* London and New York: Oxford University Press, 1983.
Locke, H. *A Bibliographical Catalogue of the Writings of Sir Arthur Conan Doyle,* 1879–1928. Tunbridge Wells, England: D. Webster, 1928.

2. Critical Studies—Books
Baring-Gould, William S. *Sherlock Holmes of Baker Street.* New York: Clarkson N. Potter, 1962. An exhaustive and informative biography of Holmes demonstrates the phenomenon of the "Sherlockian" writings.
Barzun, Jacques, and Wendell Hertig Taylor. *A Catalogue of Crime.* New York, 1971. A comprehensive, annotated bibliography of detective fiction from the beginnings to the late 1960s. Perceptive comments on Holmes.
Batho and Dobree, eds. *The Victorians and After 1830–1914.* New York:

Robert McBride & Co., 1938. Good on the romantic writers associated with Doyle, notably Stevenson and Kipling. Short critical essay
on Doyle as a writer of romance is deprecatory, asserting only that
"Rodney Stone at least attains a very high level of action."

Cawelti, John G. *Adventure, Mystery, and Romance.* Chicago and London:
University of Chicago Press, 1976. Still the best book on interpreting
the phenomenon of formulaic stories, in particular the detective story.
Suggestive discussion of Holmes linking crime to the middle-class
family in late Victorian England.

Cruse, Amy. *After the Victorians.* London: Allen & Unwin, 1938. Extensive
references to Doyle, including Doyle's views on other novelists.

Eco, Umberto, and Thomas Sebeok, eds. *The Sign of Three: Dupin, Holmes,
Peirce,* Bloomington, Ind.: Indiana University Press, 1983. A collection of ten essays in which semioticians decode and disclose the
juxtapositions between the life and work of the logician Charles Peirce
and the methods employed by Sherlock Holmes. Penetrating and
perceptive, this book suggests to critics of Holmes in particular and
of detectives in general, the many areas of inquiry still to be under-
taken.

Ernst, B. M. L., and Hereward Carrington. *Houdini and Conan Doyle: The
Story of a Strange Friendship.* New York: A and C Bono, 1932. The
complicated relationship between the illusionist Harry Houdini and
Doyle documented by their extensive correspondence. Provides first-
hand evidence of the extent of Doyle's credulity as well as his strict
sense of morality. Excellent.

Gibson, John Michael, and Richard Lancelyn Green, eds. *The Unknown
Conan Doyle: Essays on Photography.* New York: Secker & Warburg,
1982. Collection of light and lively essays on photography, written
by Doyle for the *British Journal of Photography* in the 1880s. Useful
as social history.

Gillis, James M. *False Prophets.* New York: Macmillan Co., 1927. A
Christian defends Doyle's attack on the Church. The chapter on Doyle
as a Spiritualist prophet summarizes the charges leveled at the author
in the later years of his life.

Hall, Trevor. *Sherlock Holmes and His Creator.* London: Duckworth, 1978.
Series of essays representing the continuing debate between the faithful followers of the Baker Street Canon and the rest of the world.
Fortunately, the mock-scholarly tone is often set aside here so that
"Conan Doyle and Spiritualism" is a noteworthy, well-researched look
at the writer's frame of mind when he became an adherent. Hall
ultimately understands Doyle's embracing of the faith, but he also
quotes extensively—in material not generally used—from those who
find Doyle's position indefensible.

Haycraft, Howard. *Murder for Pleasure: The Life and Times of the Detective Story.* New York and London: Appleton, Century Co., 1941. In spite of all the recent works on the subject, this is still the best history of the genre. Includes a seminal chapter on Holmes.

————, ed. *The Art of the Mystery Story.* New York: Simon & Schuster, 1946. An intelligent and helpful compilation of the most important essays devoted to detective fiction. Includes essays by Dorothy Sayers, G.K. Chesterton, Vincent Starrett, Joseph Wood Krutch, and Marjorie Nicholson.

Knox, Ronald A. *Essays in Satire.* London: Sheed & Ward, 1928. A structural analysis of the Holmes stories. Hard to read, as the writing attempts the kind of facetiousness endemic to the Holmesians, but worth reading if only for the identification of the eleven segments in *A Study in Scarlet.*

Leibow, Ely. *Dr. Joe Bell: Model for Sherlock Holmes.* Bowling Green, Ohio: Bowling Green University Popular Press, 1982. Biography of Doyle's famous medical school teacher. Leibow settles what is surely one of the sillier literary conflicts, namely: Was Dr. Bell the model for Holmes? Doyle's correspondence with Bell—reproduced here—and with members of his own family, seems to leave little room for doubt.

McQueen, Ian. *Sherlock Holmes Detected: The Problem of the Long Stories.* Newton Abbot: David & Charles, 1974. Analyses of the four Holmes novels.

Murch, A. E. *The Development of the Detective Novel.* New York: Philosophical Library, 1958. A solid work on the history and development of the genre; particularly good on the nineteenth century with a lively chapter on Doyle.

Ousby, Ian. *Bloodhounds of Heaven.* Cambridge, Mass.: Harvard University Press, 1976. A contemporary, scholarly study of the detective story with excellent chapters on Dickens, Collins, and Doyle.

Parek, Leroy. *Watteau's Shepherds: The Detective Novel in Britain 1914–1940.* Bowling Green, Ohio: Bowling Green University Press, 1979. Doyle and Holmes used in early chapters. Interestingly, the rise of the detective story is linked to the juvenile paper and schoolboy novel. A particularly important link in relation to Doyle who wrote both kinds of stories with equal gusto.

Peterson, Audrey. *Victorian Masters of Mystery: From Wilkie Collins to Conan Doyle.* New York: Frederic Ungar, 1984. The final chapter on Doyle discusses Doyle as the detective that he was in the George Edalji case. Adds nothing to what has been stated earlier about this aspect of the author's life.

Redmond, Donald A. *Sherlock Holmes: A Study in Sources.* Kingston, Ont., Canada: McGill-Queens University Press, 1982. As its title suggests, with an emphasis on the names used in the Holmes stories. Bibliography indispensable to all Sherlockians.

Rodin, Alvin E., and Jack D. Kay, *Medical Casebook of Doctor Arthur Conan Doyle: From Practitioner to Sherlock Holmes and Beyond.* Melbourne, Fla. Robert E. Krieger Publishing Company, 1984. A comprehensive account of all Doyle's medical writings. Written to demonstrate the extent and depth of his medical concerns as they appear in all his work. Fine, well-researched biographical information.

Routley, Erik. *The Puritan Pleasures of the Detective Story.* London: Gollancz, 1972. An informed analysis of reader fascination with Holmes. Also a much-needed critical discussion of Doyle as a writer of romance, linking the detective story to the genre of romance.

Sayers, Dorothy L. *Unpopular Opinions.* London: Gollancz, 1946. A collection of Miss Sayers's classic essays including those about Holmes and Watson. Excellent.

Shreffler, Philip A., ed. *The Baker Street Reader; Cornerstone Writings about Sherlock Holmes.* Westport, Conn. and England: Greenwood Press, 1984. A recent compilation of the most famous "Sherlockian" essays drawn from a wide variety of sources and spanning a period of fifty years.

Starrett, Vincent, ed. *221B: Studies in Sherlock Holmes, by Various Hands.* New York: Macmillan Co., 1940. Early collection of important essays about Holmes and Watson by the acknowledged expert on that subject. Starrett is always readable and informative.

Stevenson, Lionel. *The English Novel: A Panorama.* Cambridge, Mass.: Houghton Mifflin Co. [The Riverside Press], 1960. Thought provoking and critically stimulating account of the time, but unfortunately it only relates Doyle briefly to the other writers of romance.

Symons, Julian. *Mortal Consequences: From the Detective Story to the Crime Novel: A History.* London: Faber & Faber, 1972. Indispensable study of the form. Notable for sensible stand against what he calls "the tedious pieces" on Holmes's life, education, habits, etc.: "By emphasizing and enlarging the myth of Holmes, they tend to obscure Conan Doyle's real and considerable achievement."

Walker, Dale. *Jack London, Sherlock Holmes and Sir Arthur Conan Doyle.* Amsterdam, N.Y.: Alvin S. Fick, 1974. Reprint. Bloomington, Ind.: Gaslight Publications, 1981. Although Walker tries to demonstrate the literary kinship that existed between the two authors, the most convincing points are those describing Doyle's kinship with the group of American Spiritualists (London's relatives) who believed in London's "return" from the dead.

Watson, Colin. *Snobbery With Violence.* New York: St. Martin's Press, 1971. Study of detective story with innumerable references to Doyle and Holmes. Emphasis on class influence and connections makes this study different and important.

Waugh, Charles G., and Martin H. Greenberg, eds. *The Best Science Fiction of Arthur Conan Doyle.* Carbondale, Ill.: Southern Illinois University Press: 1981. Incisive introduction by George E. Slusser to Doyle's scientific romances, with brief but intelligent comments on all the Challenger stories.

3. Critical Studies—Articles

Barolsky, Paul. "The Case of the Domesticated Aesthete." *Virginia Quarterly Review* 60(3) (1984):438–52. Sees Holmes as a character typical of the fin de siecle—an aesthete, but overlooks first, that Holmes combines both meditative aesthete and active hero, and, second, that the aesthete side of Holmes declines over the publication of the stories.

Campbell, James L. "Sir Arthur Conan Doyle." In *Science Fiction Writers; Critical Studies of the Major Authors From the Early 19th Century to the Present Day,* edited by E.F. Bleiler. New York: Scribner's, 1982. Valuable essay. Brief, but pertinent analysis of all the Challenger stories. Draws attention to the largely overlooked long short story "The Maricot Deep," showing how Doyle sees technology aligned with materialism as leading to moral decay.

Clausen, Christopher. "Sherlock Holmes, Order, and the Late-Victorian Mind." *Georgia Review* 38(1) (Spring 1984):104–23. The Holmes canon is a "largely overlooked source for the study of late-Victorian ideas, attitudes and culture." Excellent scholarly essay linking desire for social order and middle-class fears of crime to creation of Holmes.

Farell, Kirby. "Heroism, Culture, and Dread in *The Sign of Four.*" *Studies in the Novel* 16(1) (Spring 1984):32–51. Doyle's idea about death and Holmes's "power over death" provide the structure that underlies the more obvious theme of crime and detection in the novel. Initial comparison of Holmes to Faust is weak, but the emphasis on the parallelism of "evil" couple, Small and Tonga, and the "good" couple, Holmes and Watson, is provoking and intelligent.

Ferguson, Paul F. "Narrative Vision in *The Hound of the Baskervilles.*" *Clues: A Journal of Detection* 1(2) (Fall–Winter 1983):24–30. Good essay demonstrating narrative, design, and intention in *The Hound of the Baskervilles.*

Hall, Trevor. "Sherlock Holmes: The Higher Criticism." Leeds, England: W.S. Maney & Son, 1971. For those who take pleasure in the idea that Holmes was a living person, this lecture, a parody of scholarly lectures, summarizes the debates that have bedeviled the "Higher Criticism" of the literature of Baker Street.

Jackson, Paul R. "*Pale Fire* and Sherlock Holmes." *Studies in American Fiction* 10(1) (Spring 1982):101–5. References to Holmes as they

appear in Nabokov's work. Draws attention to the important position
that the detective, as a reader of signs, holds for many modern novelists.

Meikle, Jeffrey. " 'Over There': Arthur Conan Doyle and Spiritualism."
Library Chronicle of the University of Texas 8 (1974):23–37. Historical
approach to Doyle's Spiritualism, discussing the changes that occurred
in the one-time simple adherent, leading to Doyle's stance as prophet
and teacher of millions.

4. Biographies

Carr, John Dickson. *The Life of Sir Arthur Conan Doyle*. New York: Harper,
1949. The definitive biography of Arthur Conan. As Carr had access
to Doyle's papers on an unprecedented scale, this book is filled with
information that is unavailable elsewhere, although many of the "reported" conversations and scenes are actually fictionalized.

Doyle, Adrian Conan. *The True Conan Doyle*. New York: Coward-McCann,
1946. A defense of his father written in response to what the Doyle
family regarded as Hesketh Pearson's unjust biography. This short
study is so defensive of Doyle that it raises more questions than it
answers.

Edwards, Owen Dudley. *The Quest for Sherlock Holmes*. Edinburgh: Main-
stream Publishing, 1983. Covers Doyle's first twenty-three years with
an epilogue that takes us up to *A Study in Scarlet*. Too much information about dates, times, and origin of names in the Holmes stories.
Interesting speculation about the effects of the author's father's al-
coholism on Doyle's life and work.

Hardwick, Michael, and Mollie Hardwick. *The Man Who Was Sherlock
Holmes*. Garden City, N.Y.: Doubleday & Co., 1964. Particularly
sound on the later stages of Doyle's life. Some new information,
which leads the authors to some persuasive speculations, including
their contention that Doyle lost an offer of a peerage because of his
unpopular opinions on Spiritualism.

Higham, Charles. *The Adventures of Conan Doyle: The Life of the Creator of
Sherlock Holmes*. New York: W. W. Norton & Co., 1976. A lively,
well-written but somewhat fanciful account of Doyle's life. Best on
the short stories of adventure and terror.

Lamond, John. *Arthur Conan Doyle; A Memoir*. Port Washington, N.Y.:
Kennikat Press, 1971. Reprint. 1972. A frankly eulogistic biography
by an intimate friend of the Doyle family with an emphasis on the
Spiritualist years and Doyle's development as a leader of the Spiritualist cause. Contains a glowing epilogue by Lady Conan Doyle.

Nordon, Pierre. *Conan Doyle; A Biography*. Translated by Frances Partridge.
London: John Murray, 1966. Combines accurate biographical information with an informative, intelligent analysis of all the author's

work. Of particular interest and help is the chapter on "The Novels of Chivalry." This is the best critical biography of Doyle.

Pearsall, Ronald. *Conan Doyle: A Biographical Solution.* New York: St. Martin's Press, 1977. Pearsall integrates biographical information with an analysis of Doyle's work, but he concentrates almost exclusively on Holmes. Common-sense approach to Doyle's character.

Pearson, Hesketh. *Conan Doyle.* London: White Lion Publishers, 1974. The Doyle family felt that this biography tarnished Doyle's reputation. While the tone is often nasty, it does serve as a foil to much that is fawning in other writings about Doyle.

Symons, Julian. *Portrait of an Artist: Conan Doyle.* London: Whizzard Press, Andre Deutsch, 1979. This small volume gives the usual information about Doyle's life plus some insightful comments about his writings. Supplemented by 122 photographs and illustrations.

Index